Come home,

Born in inner-Sydney to an alcoholic mother and an absent father, Carl Beauchamp and his brother Neville ran wild until they were taken into care. That care turned out to be a nightmare, with the boys placed in separate boys' homes, and in Carl's case in the hands of sexual predators.

The boys survived, but Carl kept the horrors he had endured secret, even from his brother, for decades. When Carl found the strength to speak out, he discovered the tragic aftermath of life in the Church of England Charlton Boys' Home for many of his fellow inmates.

Despite the adversity and the pain, Carl's story is overwhelmingly optimistic and heartwarming. It contains recollections of 1940s and '50s Sydney that will intrigue anyone who loves Newtown, Glebe and the surrounding suburbs, and is told in his own authentic voice.

Come home, you little bastards

Carl Beauchamp

Editia

All rights reserved. No part of this book may be reproduced or transmitted by any person or entity in any form or by any means, electronic or mechanical, including printing, photocopying (except under the statutory exceptions provisions of the Australian Copyright Act 1968), recording, scanning or by any information storage and retrieval system without the prior written permission of Editia. Any unauthorised distribution or use of this text may be a direct infringement of the authors' and publishers' rights and those responsible may be liable in law accordingly.

First published by Editia (editia.com) in 2016
Copyright © 2016 Carl Beauchamp
Editing: Geoff Weir
Cover design: Wendy Dawes
Foreword: Peter Jensen

The moral rights of the authors have been asserted.

National Library of Australia Cataloguing-in-Publication entry

Creator: Beauchamp, Carl, author.

Title: Come home you little bastards / Carl Beauchamp ; Geoff Weir, editor ; Wendy Dawes, cover designer.

ISBN: 9781942189947 (paperback)

Subjects: Beauchamp, Carl–Childhood and youth.
Sexually abused children–New South
Wales–Sydney–Biography.
Adult child sexual abuse victims–New South
Wales–Sydney–Biography.
Adult children of dysfunctional families–New South
Wales–Sydney–Biography.

Other Creators/Contributors:
Weir, Geoff, editor.
Dawes, Wendy, cover designer.

TO
REVEREND RAYMOND CHARLES WEIR
17 February, 1923, to 2 October, 1978
Sydney Children's Court Chaplain 1950 to 1954,
Rector St Clement's Mosman, St Thomas's Kingsgrove,
St Matthew's Manly, St Alban's Lindfield, St Jude's
Bowral; Chaplain NSW Police Force, NSW Gaols,
Citizens' Military Forces; Migrant Escort Chaplain;
Chairman of the International Nepal
Fellowship; Foundation Member of Lindfield and
Kingsgrove Rotary

As a mark of wholehearted affection and respect to a true loving man of God. He gave so much of himself to each poverty-stricken boy he escorted to Charlton and other Church of England homes throughout NSW. His compassion was overwhelming.
This book is also dedicated to others who helped me restore my faith.
Thank you Chaplain Jenni Woodhouse and Phillip Gerber of the Anglican Professional Standards Unit at St Andrew's House in Sydney, for your altruistic compassion and kindness.

Thank you for your understanding and most of all for helping me understand that the Lord was with me and is with me always, until the very end.
Thank you Archbishop Peter Jensen for your kind words and your loving gift of a Bible.
My thanks also to a compassionate Minister I met at St Peter's Anglican Church in Campbelltown, Reverend Joe Zagninski, who was filling in at the end of 2009. Thank you, Joe for the many personal prayers and for sincerely asking the Lord's help for me during my moments of anxiety, depression and emotional heartache. Thanks also for your assistance with helping me organise the Charlton reunion on 13 March, 2010, at St Peter's Church, Campbelltown.

Carl Beauchamp
Sydney, 2016

Contents

	Editor's preface	xi
	Foreword	xiii
	Introduction	xv
1.	My beginning	1
2.	Carlingford Boys' Home	15
3.	Home again	25
4.	Mates, girls and games	47
5.	Church life	59
6.	Escape attempt	63
7.	Before the Children's Court	73
8.	Life in Charlton	79
9.	The abuse	95
10.	Role of Sachisthal	109
11.	Returning home	113

12.	My first motor car and the deadly accident	123
13.	On the move again	131
14.	Army, girls and moving out at last	137
15.	Meeting Beryl again	143
16.	New beginnings	147
17.	Reflections	151
	Experiences of other Charlton inmates	163
	Acknowledgements	175
	'A very fortunate life'	179

Editor's preface

If you have ever wondered what it was like growing up in poverty in Sydney in the 1940s and '50s; how it felt being a powerless child subjected to institutionalised physical and sexual abuse; or why it is that some children not only survived such abuse but went on to live happy, fulfilling lives while many others could not, then this story of Carl's extraordinary life is a must read.

My first contact with Carl was by way of a phone call in the middle of a dinner party. He said to me: "Geoff, you don't know me but I feel I know you and your family well. I've been doing research on your Dad's life because I'm trying to get him awarded the Order of Australia. I need your help."

Three weeks later I rang Carl to tell him that, sadly, I had discovered it was not possible to be awarded the Order of Australia posthumously. A week after that, I was emotionally engulfed in hundreds of pages of text Carl had sent me describing his life growing up in abject poverty in inner Sydney and being abused in a Church of England boys' home.

Carl has written this evocative and disturbing account of his upbringing as a means of closure for himself and his family; as a testament to the other boys abused at Charlton Boys' Home and in many other institutions; and as a case study on the survival power of love through even the most horrendous circumstances. He has dedicated his book to my father, who tried to help him and other boys like him.

It has been a privilege working with Carl on his story and, in the process, getting to know such a courageous man. I trust that, in the course of editing his words, I have not diluted the integrity and power of his voice.

I would like to thank David Alexander, Andrew Butler and Geoff Sutherland for their feedback and help in editing Carl's manuscript.

Geoff Weir
2016

Foreword

I well remember how proud we were as Anglicans to be involved in the work of looking after boys through Charlton Boys' Home. Little did we know what horrors were enacted within its walls as told by the men whose stories are recorded in Carl's book.

It is a bitter story and one that can only leave you utterly dismayed at the evil done under the cloak of religion. A redeeming feature is the courage of those who have spoken up and the compassion of those like Reverend Ray Weir, Chaplain to the Boys' Home.

Another wonderful aspect of what you will read is the outcome of Carl's life, where, in moving words, he testifies to the way in which love entered his life at various points and he responded positively. However awful sin and crime are, they cannot conquer love and forgiveness.

I am so glad that my friend Carl Beauchamp has helped tell the whole story and encouraged others to speak. We have a great deal to learn from him. It is a privilege to know him.

Peter Jensen
Former Archbishop of Sydney

Introduction

As we age many important things are forgotten, and we often require something dramatic to trigger memories. Many memories are hidden and lost as a safeguard for our own sanity. If we did not possess this mechanism, our emotional stability would suffer and we would find ourselves in a deep black hole of depression, not only hurting ourselves but everyone around us. Sometimes our pain destroys everything around us so much that we dig ourselves a deeper hole, and soon find we can't get out of it.

I took a different approach. Writing this book has been my way of confronting head-on the pain and emotional traumas of my life. I believe this process has also made me a better person. Having reconciled myself to the ups and downs of my life, the good times and the bad, remembering what it is like to be unloved, to live in poverty, and to be brutalised and sexually assaulted has made me more understanding of the sufferings of others. I have been there and I know the heartache.

The writing and the recording of my upbringing and my time as an inmate at the Charlton Memorial Church of England Boys' Home in Glebe has been an ongoing project involving more than nine years of research, including speaking and writing to

Introduction

many former inmates who shared their good and bad memories with me. As these men recalled their time spent at Charlton, most of them cried tears of pain and anger as the memories flooded back.

These memories had been blocked out for a very long time. Like me, very few told their parents how they suffered. Very few told their wives. Instead their secrets remained locked away – in my case until the 2004 hearings by the Senate Community Affairs References Committee Inquiry into Children in Institutional Care, to which I gave evidence and which shone a light on how thousands of children like myself had their innocence stolen from them by people who were employed by the church to care for them and to keep them safe. Sadly, the church believed these people to be honourable men and women.

These paedophiles felt safe: while some of us spoke about our hurt to each other, the paedophiles knew that none of us had the courage to report the crimes because we were too scared of the consequences that would surely follow. While I was an inmate at Charlton, a report to the Superintendent by a six-year-old boy of being raped was not believed and for years after he was relentlessly victimised, severely punished and given the name "liar". Needless to say, most of us kept our mouths shut for fear of receiving similar never-ending punishment.

Of course, there were truly decent Christian people working at Charlton, whose only fault was they either could not see the sexual molestation going on under their noses or chose not to see it. Some of them at least had to know what was going on, but they chose to keep quiet. These people were decent human beings afraid to speak out. Evil at Charlton was triumphant because good people said and did nothing. This truism was evident to all of us boys. The sexual attacks were relentless; not only within the home, but by people who were allowed to take us to their private homes and on outings and camps. Most

Introduction

of these people had connections within the church. One was a preacher, others were associated through boys' clubs and the YMCA. Others were businessmen who made large donations to Charlton. They were all friends of Norman Sachisthal, the Superintendent at Charlton, himself an alleged paedophile, who was later awarded the OBE for his "Services to Child Welfare".

Most of us were decent, God-fearing boys who were taught that Jesus loved us. "Suffer the little children to come unto me," we were taught. We believed these words and some of us prayed in our own way, asking for help. Sadly, over time we felt we had been abandoned and many of us started to lose our faith in God. Many old Charlton boys today become very distressed at even the mention of religion. "Where was God when I needed him most to protect me from monsters?" they ask me.

I survived, as did my faith. This is the story of what happened, why it happened and how I survived it.

Carl Beauchamp
Sydney, 2016

1

My beginning

Carl Morris was 14 years and 10 months old when he was killed. He was riding his pushbike along King Street, Newtown, when he was hit by a truck. If he had not been killed at that place and time, I would not be here today to tell my story.

Carl should not have been in Sydney, only coming down from Queanbeyan to help his father Charles Morris with work. Below is the last letter that Carl ever wrote:

Dear Mum,

I received your ever-welcome letter today and also Bub's. Tell her to use a pad next time and not one of my old exercise books. I received my watch on Sunday morning, but it was not in what you'd call excellent trim, it will go smoothly for a while and then it seems to catch on a stroke, stop then start the stroke, all over again, it is losing too.
I will give a weeks notice this Friday, the ordinary fare to Sydney I was told is twenty three shillings, I don't know how much I will have because, I have to get a pair of gloves, and a few other things, maybe.
Tell Dad I'd be only too pleased to work for him. I'm not at all

surprised about Joe, he's more at home in an office than one of Dad's jobs. That woman I told you about and was over the other day and told me that if I could stick my job out till September, I could go with them in their car. They are going to Sydney for their holidays. He works at the C.O.R. I will ask them to call in and see you one day, while they are in Sydney; well I think I will have to close now.

I am the Prodigal Son,

Carl

Carl's family secured George Andrews Funeral Directors in Newtown. During the making of the funeral arrangements, Carl's sister – my mother – who was 19 at the time, met my father in the Funeral Director's office where he worked. Reg Beauchamp arranged the necessary paperwork for Carl's funeral that was set for 29 July 1935: the day after Carl's death.

The funeral was arranged with burial at Rookwood cemetery, down near the railway lines towards Lidcombe, looking up the hill to the Church of England office.

Carl was fondly called Carlie. My grandfather, Charles Morris, did all the concrete and headstone work. The headstone read: "In memory of Carl, dearly loved and only son of Charles and Kate Morris, loving brother of Bebe and Lydia, died 28th July 1935. Result of accident, aged 14 years and 10 months." Over the years I have gone to the grave and cleaned it up.

Each day after Carl's burial, my mother Bebe (her real name was Mary but she went by the names of Bebe, Val or Thelma) would call in to Andrews Funeral Parlour and see Reginald Beauchamp. It was from this moment that they started courting. They were engaged, then married on 7 November 1935 at the Methodist Church on King Street, Newtown.

MY EARLY YEARS

It soon became obvious to all that knew them that Bebe Morris and Reg Beauchamp were badly matched. Reg worked long, hard hours and had to put up with Mum's childish tantrums and infatuation for other men.

My mother's problems were other men and drink. She was a person of a very aggressive nature when drinking alcohol, and if she did not get her own way she threw childlike tantrums. A relative told me there was an incident after I was born at Newtown in 1937 where she used me as a shield, daring Reg to hit her, knowing he would have hit the baby in the process. Mum would do stupid and irresponsible things at times.

During these early days they moved from Newtown to Enfield and then later on to Erskineville. It was from here the marriage turned sour and finished up with both hating each other, like the movie *The War of the Roses*.

Reg would come home from work after a hard day at the funeral parlour, and quite naturally after washing and cleaning himself up he would expect to find an evening meal ready. Very often no meal had been cooked, because as Mum would say, she had also had a hard day looking after a "bloody whingeing child", which was me. The truth was that Mum was more interested in sitting and reading books in the sun, out on the front verandah, watching all the good-looking blokes going by. It was throughout this time, about 1940, with the Cosmopolitan Hotel opposite our house, that she started her secret drinking. Mum often had bottles of wine and beer in hidden places, so Reg would not stumble upon them. I have no doubt Reg loved my mother in the beginning at least, and Mum was truly in love with Reg. Sadly, however, Mum never changed from being a selfish and vain person, only interested in her own needs rather than anyone else's. Mum's Marilyn Monroe looks never made her a loving mother or a good wife. Instead, everything about Mum was self-gratification.

I have been told that as a baby I suffered badly from colic and that the pain would have me crying in anguish, hour after hour. I'm told that Mum would always feed me with haste and leave me with a bottle, even though she knew I was full of wind. She allowed me to cry for hours, closing the door to block out my crying, and then she would leave the house to gossip with her friends or go right up the backyard to read and sun herself. Later if she came into the house to get something with me still crying, she would handle me very roughly. No doubt I was interfering with her leisure time.

Men used to look at my mother and envy Reg. She loved this and encouraged it: every time the opportunity offered itself, she would give men the eye, the come-on. One sunny day on King Street, Newtown, whilst walking with Reg, she gave these two men the eye outside the Oxford Hotel. They turned around and said something that embarrassed and upset my father; he walked up to them and hit one of them, knocking him to the ground. My father then chased after Mum, who had continued walking. This behaviour made her day: Mum, after creating the fight, was unconcerned, quite blasé. Mum loved men fighting over her. No doubt these events made her feel wanted. I often wonder: was her own childhood so unloved?

Reg caught up with Mum and they argued and brawled all the way home, but before Reg had caught up, one of the men chased Reg and attempted to king hit him. Reg turned quickly and hit the man with a flurry of punches, which soon had him running back to his mate.

As if this was not bad enough, the fight with Mum continued as they reached my grandmother Ma Kate's house at 59 Campbell Street, Newtown. Of course this involved other members of the household and a further all-round argument took place. Reg said to Bebe: "As far as I'm concerned you can stay here with your mother: don't bother coming home." Ma Kate Morris always took Mum's side and never had much time for Reg. Charlie Morris, my Grandad, thought a great deal of Reg, and in his own way tried to help the young married couple as best he could. Sometimes he would share his last few shillings with them. "I've never ever heard a bad word said against Reg Beauchamp," Charlie would say. Charlie was kind and gentle, a small man with little hair like a grey halo; he loved smoking his cigars. He wore his pocket watch on a chain that was contained in a pocket in his vest, which he always wore.

So Reg would take off and leave Mum at Ma Kate's, but only for a few hours. After that he would come back begging. Nevertheless, Mum would never change her ways, fighting then making up, like a cycle round and round, over and over again. Reg thought the world of Mum and loved her so much in those early days, but he could not stand her bad attitude. Loving her so much, it was Reg always doing the giving.

If they had stayed together much longer than they did, they would have killed each other, as sure as night turns to day: they were at each other's throats every single day. Mum's attitude and my father's acrimonious bad temper were a recipe for total disaster: they truly were not compatible. Reg often got into trouble for hitting first without thinking.

It was while living at Enfield that an event took place that landed Reg in court. In those days the house owner would personally collect the rent. One such day, the owner called and knocked on the front door. As he put his hand on the door, it opened and he saw me standing there in the hallway with a pencil in my hand, drawing on the newly painted wall. I was only three years old, but the owner was not going to stand for this type of vandalism of his house. He walked in, grabbed the pencil out of my hand and struck me very hard across the head. I fell to the floor and started crying uncontrollably.

Next thing Mum came running in from her favourite spot up the back yard, where she had been reading in the sun. She had an abusive argument with the owner. "Don't you ever lay a hand on my child again," she said. "Any more wrecking my house and I'll throw you out," retaliated the owner.

That afternoon my father came home for lunch. I told him a man had come to the house and that he had hit me. At first he was not concerned about the man hitting me. But after sitting down and thinking about it, Reg went to find my mother.

"Who was the man here today who you've been playing around with? A man is at work, working his guts out, and here you are playing around. I've had it," he said. "Who is he? I'll knock his brains out."

They were both experts at the use of foul language, which made great entertainment for the neighbours and busybodies of the street. Sometimes I believe they carried on with their horrible behaviour to impress the neighbours, with each outdoing the other with the foulest language one could imagine.

My mother, equal to the battle at hand, would give Reg as much as he gave her. Mum would pick up anything to throw; Reg in his temper would put his fist through walls or break furniture. If he did not take his anger out on these things, his violence would have seen my mother dead, with him in gaol and me without parents.

After things had calmed down a little, my mother was able to tell Reg exactly what happened. Reg was then in a new rage. "Nobody touches my kid," he yelled, and then said to Mum: "Where were you?" He then accused Bebe of being out the backyard with some bloke, and then the blue would start all over again. "You're nothing but a cheap slut, just a whore, and you will never change."

Things ignited on the next rent collection day. Reg stayed home from work, waiting eagerly to catch the bloke who hit me. A knock came to the front door. Reg opened it and there was the owner. "Good morning, Mr Beauchamp," he said. Before he had finished speaking, Reg hit the landlord fair and square in the middle of his face. Blood was squirting from the man's nose as he crashed to the ground. Reg continued his angry advance on him with great aggression, the landlord dragging himself along the ground, trying to put as much distance as possible between them. The landlord jumped up, running to the front fence, telling Reg: "I'll see you in gaol and out of this house." As he fled up the street, Reg followed him yelling: "Come back here you coward child basher. Next time I'll kill you."

With so much noise, all our immediate neighbours had been gathering out the front of the house, with everyone urging Reg on, calling out "chase the bastard, Reg" and "kill the bastard, Reg" and much more, all on the side of Reg. This is the Australian way: they were barracking for the underdog. There was so much hate towards the landlord who had no sympathy for the tenants, and had evicted many.

Reg was used to being in trouble with the police. "Trouble" could have been his second name. Reg knew that the police would soon be paying him a visit. He was not to be disappointed. Arrive they did, in very fast time, and Reg was arrested and bundled into the Black Maria, then taken to Newtown Police Station and charged. In court later he was fined £5 for the assault of the owner.

Reg was in a rage over being fined, and then came the notice to quit. Reg had been expecting this and had already had his furniture moved to another address. In an empty house, Reg did not have long to wait before the landlord arrived with the notice to quit. It appears the landlord was a slow learner: as he proceeded to hand Reg the notice, bang bang, right in the middle of his face, and down he went, out cold. Reg stepped over his unconscious body, closed the door and then got on his motorbike and sidecar and drove off, as calm as you please and as cool as a cucumber. Leaving without paying the rent pleased Reg immensely. No doubt this was again reported but having moved on, the police probably gave up on Reg.

And so to another house, this time 39 Albert Street, Erskineville. The move here had all the ingredients for more trouble with Mum: we were right opposite the Cosmopolitan Hotel. Next door but one was the local grocery shop, on the corner of Charles and Albert streets. Mr Bourke was the grocer. If you did not have money, you could 'book up' (put it on credit). On the opposite corner was King's Fish Shop, which sold greasy fish. The Cosmopolitan Hotel was run by Moira Hartigan, the first female licensed publican in Sydney. Her brother Tommy Hartigan was the local starting price (SP) bookmaker. The closing hours were six every weekday evening. They also opened for a few hours on Saturday, closing at midday.

Tommy Hartigan was well liked and would operate from one house to another, keeping one step ahead of the police. He would pay the people of each house a good rental for the Saturday use. I recall that Tommy at one time or another used nearly every house in Albert Street. He used to come down each Saturday from his Pennant Hills pig farm. Our house, a double storey terrace house, had been used here and there. All the terraces in our block had access to the back service lane, which was good for Tommy as punters' comings and goings were less noticeable. Tommy always had a lookout to warn of police presence.

Moira Hartigan ran a respectable business at the Cosmopolitan Hotel. In those days, a separate room was set aside for women drinkers, called the 'Hen Pen'. It did not take Mum long to join the Hen Pen set and soon she was spending her afternoons drinking. Needless to say, our lives suffered as a result. Seldom were meals cooked, and money soon ran out due to Mum's drinking. If it was a hot day and she could not be bothered going over to the Hen Pen bar, Mum would give me this large glass jug with money and have me – a five-year-old little kid – go over and beckon one of her boyfriends or other men friends to the hotel door and ask them to fill the jug for Mum. Mum always warned me: "Don't let Moira Hartigan see you."

In those days the people doing bar work had no access to the till. Moira had a special area set up in the hotel centre where she had her cash register. The barmaids would take the money from the customer, give it to Moira and then return the change to the customer. If they received a tip they had to give it to Moira and she placed it in a jar for them to divide up after work.

Most of the men were very happy to do Mum a favour. God only knows how many favours she did them in return. Often when handing me the beer they would give me a penny for myself. I then had to walk slowly back to our house carrying the beer jug. Sometimes it was too full and I would stop and drink some so as not to waste any. Nobody could say I was stupid: I liked the beer taste.

Many a time when Mum had no money for beer, she would force open the gas meter box and take money from it, but of course this would have to be repaid. Well one day the meter collection man arrived before Mum had a chance to pay back what she had taken, so she said: "Someone has broken into the house." Did they believe her? Mum and her smile and good looks would even convince the devil.

Sometimes while I was waiting for the man to fill Mum's jug with beer, some of the men in the pub, feeling sorry for me, would put some money in my hands, saying: "Don't let your mother have it: buy some lollies." I felt like a king as I later chose various lollies at the corner shop, choosing carefully, one of those and some of these. It brought a smile to my face. Mum was greedy and if she knew I had some money she would take it from me.

Mum then started bringing a few of her drinking friends – mostly women – home each day when Reg was at work. They would sit around all afternoon talking, singing and drinking. When they emptied one jug they would go over to the hotel or have me go over and have their men friends refill the jug, over and over again all afternoon. Needless to say, housework never got done and meals were not prepared. Mum was often too pissed to care. As the housekeeping money was being used for Mum's pleasure, my brothers and I became much like the children under the control of Fagan in a Charles Dickens' Oliver Twist: no shoes and with the backsides out of our pants, we never had sheets and only a few threadbare, worn-out army blankets.

For a long time after the owner Mr Isles had fumigated our house, we also had no mattress to sleep on nor a pillow, because all these had been burnt down the backyard to prevent a reinfestation of bugs and fleas. So Mum placed old newspapers over the bed wire. They were very uncomfortable to sleep on.

Well with all the drinking, it did not take Mum and her friends long to start fighting and become enemies. I recall one instance with the Hardman family next door at 37 Albert Street. Old Mrs Hardman had two daughters. One was bitchy Agnes. The other was a good-looking redhead who was a little jealous of Mum. She had been one of Mum's close drinking friends, but they had a falling out over the men giving Mum more attention than her.

One day an argument using extreme foul language was heard everywhere out in the street: another day of entertainment for the busybodies of Albert Street. I soon learnt what swear words were all about: my Mum invented lots of foul words. Eventually Mum turned it into a violent brawl in the middle of the street. Mum fought the Hardman women. Soon she had the mother, who she called "Bitchface", on the ground, punching and pulling her hair out. She had Agnes on her back and the old Hardman mother ran inside nursing a broken nose, blood everywhere. Mum shook Agnes off, got up and smashed Agnes once in the centre of her face. She fell to the ground and Mum kept punching her head. Shortly a few of the hotel drinkers decided everyone had had enough free entertainment. They grabbed Mum, pulling her away. I tell you, these men were brave: as they released their grip on Mum, she swung a wild punch which hit one quite hard and he backed away, retreating back to the hotel and calling Mum a maniac. "Keep away from that blonde whore: she's lost her mind," he told his mates.

Someone had called the police. When they arrived, everything was quiet: all combatants had retreated to the safety of their homes. The police could hear swearing behind the respective doors of the female warriors, so they knocked on our door, but Mum would not answer, and eventually the police drove off.

DIVORCE

This battle provided the ingredients for Mum and Dad to have one last fight. Mum had taken up with Flossie Forest, who lived six houses up in the next block near the John Street corner but two, and they had become real good drinking mates; there was also another lady, Sylvia, who was only a learner drinker. Sylvia lived in Campbell Street, Newtown, and worked for the Post Master General's Department. Sylvia liked me a lot and was always hugging me and kissing me and touching me all over my body. I liked Sylvia: she made me feel real good and she always gave me a few pennies. Often whilst my father was at work Mum and some of her friends – Flossie, Sylvia, Joyce or Agnes – would take men up to the bedrooms. I often walked in on them doing it: I would watch and they never paid any attention to me being present. At first I was confused but after a while I knew what was going on.

Mum just could not get enough sex. No matter how many times Mum denied having sex with other men, my father Reg always had doubts about her faithfulness.

One day, Mum had placed Neville and myself in bed and when we were asleep she sneaked out to meet Bill, her latest boyfriend. He was a conductor on the 300 bus that went from Erskineville to Sydney. Her girlfriends Joyce and Flossie were both having extramarital affairs with the bus driver. The bus would stop outside our house and Mum and one or other of her girlfriends would get on the bus, with the driver stopping under the MacDonaldtown railway bridge. This was only a hundred yards from our house but was secluded. All lights in the bus were switched off and here on this winter evening, they all cuddled up and had sex.

Our father had come home earlier than expected and found us asleep, but Mum was nowhere to be found. Some time later Mum came in with an excuse that Reg accepted. However, a few weeks later as he came home, Agnes Hardman – the brave warrior next door – called out: "Reg, have you a spare moment?" Reg said: "Yes, what do you want?" She said: "I don't want to cause trouble, but Bebe has been having an ongoing affair with Bill the driver's conductor on the 300 bus." She added: "She and her girlfriend only a short time ago jumped on the bus and on the return trip parked as usual under MacDonaldtown railway bridge." She then swiftly departed inside. So much for her not wanting to cause trouble!

Reg was in a mad rage and he waited for the bus to arrive. Shortly it came around the bend. Reg jumped aboard and ran to the driver, placed one arm around the driver's neck and punched him with the other, over and over. The bus was all over the road.

Come home, you little bastards

As it came to the tunnel bend at MacDonaldtown railway station the driver lost control and the bus nearly rolled over.

By this time the conductor, who was upstairs with Mum, had raced down and punched Reg. Reg turned and punched him, leaving the conductor a bloody mess on the floor. The driver had now stopped the bus and run away, and in the other direction ran Mum and her girlfriends. The bus was damaged – in his rage Dad had broken some of the windows – and the conductor was dripping blood all over the place, but no driver could be seen.

My father then returned home to confront Mum, but before he had a chance to do so the Newtown Police arrived. They charged him and placed him in a cell. Reg later came before the Magistrate charged with assault. The Magistrate must have felt sorry for Reg and only fined him, with a severe warning to keep the peace. My Uncle Seth prior to his death had told me the Magistrate had been going to send Reg to gaol but took pity on him because he blamed Mum for causing all these problems. This Newtown Magistrate was no fool.

Mum had gone into hiding, but Reg eventually found her. By this time he had calmed down. He knew it was no use continuing with the relationship. Well Reg then packed all his personal belongings and moved out, leaving my little brother Neville and me with Mum. I was about five at this time and Neville was three. In later years Dad said he had no choice in the matter as Mum had full custody sanctioned by the Court. I don't know if that was true.

And so Neville and I were left to many more years of neglect and violence. Always hungry, cold and sick, often with boils and suffering malnutrition to such an extent that we were very lethargic a lot of the time. The drunken sex orgies continued, and we became even more neglected. Every weekend was a love-in at 39 Albert Street, Erskineville. Some neighbours, like the Thorne family, called our house "The Whorehouse".

Carl Beauchamp

With Reg gone, Mum had to get a job. Soon she was working for JJ Hoelie, a factory that made bakelite light switches, in Darlington. This now gave her a new wave of friends, men and women, and new and bigger weekend drunken sex parties, which took place in full view of Neville and myself. We were learning too fast about what adults did together.

2
Carlingford Boys' Home

It was becoming very obvious that Neville and I were just a hindrance to Mum's frivolous lifestyle, and sure enough it was not long before she took us by bus and train on a journey to Epping, then another bus to Carlingford Church of England Boys' Home, where I was to stay. Neville was placed in Havilah Infants Home. In hindsight it was the best thing for us, but we were just little kids and although we had been living in hell, we could not believe she would give up on us. I was seven and Neville was four years old.

I could not believe what Mum was doing to us. One thing for sure: it was not for love of us that she sent us to the Boys' Homes. It was just a way to get rid of us. Mum was only happy when with her mates and never-ending string of boyfriends.

I remember it as if it was only yesterday. She had packed our very few belongings in a suitcase for the journey, then on arrival at Carlingford we walked across the well manicured lawns and into the main building. We still did not realise what was happening: Mum never said a word. We went into an office and were greeted by a Mr Hill. Soon they were talking about us as if we were not there, then Mr Hill spoke to me, telling me how I'd enjoy living at the Boys' Home. But I still could not comprehend that Mum was giving us away: I burst out crying in pain and so too did little Neville. Even today, near 70 years later, as I remember it, I still feel the pain and hurt that erupted that day so long ago. This was the greatest pain I have ever experienced: never have I been as hurt as I was on that summer day in January 1945.

The tears fell from my eyes like rain, my face was all wet as was my shirt, my mouth was dry, my face was tight and my heart was beating ever so fast. Neville was crying too, but he still did not understand anything. Well by this time Matron Hill had come into the office and they both tried to reassure me that I'd be all right and Neville would be well looked after with the infants in Havilah.

No matter what they said and how kind they were, it did not help. Then Mum gave me a quick kiss on the cheek and left, with the door closing behind her and Neville. Matron then proceeded to talk to me about the Home. She took hold of my hand, directing me to walk beside her, out of the office and across the neat lawns to a small cottage, which was to be my new home. As we walked out the door, I caught sight of Mum and Neville in the distance. This was too much: I broke away from Matron Hill and ran to where they had been, but they were gone. Where were they? I cried. Now Matron Hill had caught up to me as I exploded in pain and fell on the grass, crying uncontrollably. I just wanted to die.

Matron eventually helped me up. My legs felt so weak. I've never forgotten how she squeezed me tight with both arms, holding me close, and kissed my forehead and ran her hand through my hair. Matron Hill tried so hard to comfort me. No doubt she understood my suffering, as she had probably confronted the same heartbreak with many other young children. But all her kindness could not stop my pain, which was with me every day of my time at Carlingford Boys' Home.

Through the eyes of a seven-year-old, everything seems so big. Carlingford Boys' Home to me was huge, although many years later while on a visit it seemed so small. Matron Hill took me over to the cottage that was to be my home for the next 12 months. I was placed in the care of the "cottage mother", whose name I have since forgotten. I was shown my bed: it was so beautiful in a nice dormitory and was spotlessly clean. I had a small side table, and everything appeared to be green, including the bed covers and curtains. I had never in my life seen such beautiful things and everything so clean and tidy. The whole cottage had shining floors.

The cottage mother showed me around then gave me new clothing, some for school and some for ordinary wear. She gave me underwear: this was new, I'd never had underwear before. She showed me my pegs in the bathroom for my towel and face washer and a place for my toothbrush. Again everything was green and the wooden floors were polished with a few scattered rugs here and there.

I was left to myself the rest of the day. I recall walking into the clean, sparkling washroom where my thoughts again returned to Mum and Neville. Once again I could not control my emotions and burst out crying, and the pain and tightness began all over again. I don't know how long I cried. The next thing I heard was the cottage mother calling my name as she woke me on the washroom floor. Obviously I had gone to sleep. I had no idea how long I had been there, but the sun was still shining through the windows.

The other children had arrived back from school and it was tea time. Everyone in the cottage marched in an orderly fashion to the dining room. Here I saw for the first time everyone from every cottage, big boys and smaller boys like me. We all went to our respective tables. It all appeared so big to me and I was a little frightened and insecure, a scared and confused little boy. The hurt was still with me, and I was not feeling well. I felt as if I was going to vomit.

The food looked very good with a nice aroma but I could not bring myself to eat any of it. Kind Matron Hill came over to where I was seated and placed her hand on my shoulder. She assured me the food was fine. She told me she would see me the next day as she had a pair of shoes for me my mother had left in the office.

When she left I could feel the pain starting to engulf me again. I could not control my emotions. I cried my heart out and was struggling to get my breath. All the other little boys and bigger boys were watching me and I became scared. After the meal was over, everyone moved outside. Here we were directed to the church chapel: I can still visualise how beautiful it was. Matron sat next to me and every time I looked up, her kind eyes were watching me ever so closely, with her arm around my back.

A man who was a preacher said a few words from his big Bible and then everyone stood up and sang a hymn, which I had heard at Erskineville Church: it was *There Is A Green Hill Far Away*. I did not know all the words of that hymn, but it has always been firmly entrenched in my memory as one of my favourites. I fell in love with the Home Chapel and tried my best never to miss a Service. I always felt secure in this Chapel; here I was being able to put my suffering out of my mind as I recalled Matron's eyes watching me that first day.

I had been going to Erskineville School before entering Carlingford, and had become used to my teacher, who I loved: she was kind and interested in us little boys. I had also seen the visiting school nurse a few times who knew we were ill and malnourished, and my teacher knew this also. So now in a new environment I had to start a new school. The first day for me at Carlingford School was a frightening experience, but I soon overcame the fear as I learned how things were done. At morning play there were jam sandwiches for the Home kids and at lunch a box with a few sandwiches of jam or Marmite and a piece of fruit. I still remember the unique smell and taste of our lunches. I made friends and sometimes boys from private homes would ask about swapping sandwiches. Often they would give in return a piece of fruit or a piece of cake. There were also date palm trees in the school playground, and we used to eat the dates that fell to the ground. They were great.

When we arrived back at the Home after school, the cottage mother would have a sandwich and glass of fresh milk, which came from the Home's own dairy. The fresh milk was wonderful: it was the best milk I had ever had. Even to this day I can still taste the cream that lay on the top of the milk. After this we were allowed to play around outside. It was forbidden to go outside the main gates. I tried to keep away from the front fence, because every time I saw a bus passing it would bring back memories and I'd finish up crying.

I remember one little boy whose father a little later was killed in the war by the Japanese. He called me Carlie. He said to me: "Don't cry – we will see our daddies again one day." I said I did not have a daddy because he had left us a few years ago.

This little boy's father had been reported missing in action. He had been given the book *Blinky Bill* the last time he saw his Dad. His father read it to him before he went away to the war. Sometimes this boy would let me look at his book. That was how I first heard of Blinky Bill, who became my favourite book character. I had no books and I always thought he was so lucky, but in hindsight I was really the lucky one as he allowed me to hold his book that his departed dad had given him.

One day I came upon this boy crying and he told me about

his Daddy having been killed by the Japanese when he was a prisoner of war. I felt so sad to see him crying. I knew the pain he was suffering and I sat down next to him and was crying with him. Watching this little boy cry I felt his pain like it was mine. I knew better than most how he was feeling: I had lost my Mum; he had lost his Dad. The one consolation for me was one day I would see my Mum again; he would only have a memory of his Dad.

The cottage mother heard us crying. She told us his Dad was a very brave soldier who gave his life for all of us. She helped us up and took us inside and spoke to us kindly, as if she knew our sadness. She gave us both a hug then walked away, not wanting us to see the tears in her own eyes.

Some nights our cottage mother would sit in the playroom on the floor with us in a circle. She would read letters out loud for all to hear from mums and dads or grandparents, some from dads all over the world, fighting for our freedom. There was always so much love in the letters, read by the cottage mother. She would read us stories and we would sing songs about Jesus like: "Jesus loves me, yes I know, for the Bible tells me so," and for a very vulnerable boy like me, the songs gave me hope. Then she would have all of us say a quiet prayer to ourselves. My prayer was always the same, asking Jesus to bring my Mum back to me. Then she would say a prayer for all of us to hear and then take us all to bed, checking we were all tucked in, nice and warm.

One day our cottage mother asked us: "Would you like to have your own personal gardens?" She said the big boys have gardens and so shall we. She said the boy who has the best garden would get a prize. I made a garden about six feet by six feet. An older boy helped me dig it up and shape it. I grew a pumpkin vine from seeds given to me. I do not know which boy or boys received the prize, but I enjoyed looking after my garden. I used to try copying the big boys, and soon my garden was looking nice and neat with big sloping sides.

Some time later as I was watering and taking out weeds a bigger boy came along and hit me. He called me a crybaby. This same boy often used to torment me, like the time I had gone to my seat for breakfast with him sitting nearby. As we came out from breakfast, we were each handed one slice of fried bread, which we received each day. I was about to take a bite when up comes this big bully and grabs my piece of fried bread and throws it away. Not content with that, he then starts punching me and I fell down crying in pain and cut my face on hitting the rough walkway.

Matron Hill saw the whole episode, and swiftly told the boy to report to Mr Hill's office for punishment. Once again this angel of a lady was there for me, so kind: more like the mother I never had.

The bully left me alone after this and never bothered me again. Then one day at school I saw him fighting another boy, who was hurting him real bad: our bullyboy had blood over his face. Everyone had crowded around and soon the teachers were dragging them apart, then up to the Principal's office for punishment. In those days the teacher could cane you for punishment. He received six of the best.

By rights, I should have been delighted that the Home bully had met his match, but I was not. In fact I felt sorry for him, because I think he came from a family where he was constantly abused with violence, with his bully boy ways being all he knew. On our way home after school, I told him I was sorry he got hurt. Then he surprised me by saying it was his fault, having pinched the other boy's cake out of his school bag.

To make it double jeopardy, when we got back to Carlingford this boy was called to Mr Hill's office and punished again.

After all this, the bully boy became my friend. He told me

to call him Bill, which he liked better than William. He would help me with my garden. He did not have a garden because he did not want one when first asked. He was stronger than me and did the hard digging. He changed his mealtime seat and moved next to me, and as strange as it may appear he became a vastly different boy and his bully tactics became lost in the past. I believe me saying sorry was what changed him: he knew I was truly sorry he got bashed up. Sorry is said to be the hardest word for many people to say. One day he apologised to me for previously hurting me. He said: "Sorry Carlie and thanks for being kind to me."

Well, as I grew more used to the Home, I was to see many other bully boys who took great delight in hurting other boys they thought they could torment by calling them names, coming from behind and punching them, hiding towels or toothbrushes or stealing a favourite book. But the worst thing was tormenting very small emotional boys who wet the bed. The cottage mother was very understanding and never made a fuss about bedwetting, but if she heard anyone belittling another boy over wetting the bed she would get cranky and give these boys the job of polishing the wooden floors.

In my time at the Home, visiting was on a Saturday afternoon after lunch, and on the second week I was in the Home my Mum paid me a visit. I was up at the front gate watching all the buses come and go and watching all the other boys with their parents coming and going. Then all of a sudden I caught sight of Mum: she had blonde hair, which was easy to sight. "Holy Moses," I cried, as I was so overjoyed. I ran up to Mum and threw myself into her arms. With sheer joy I cried as I held her ever so tight. I was so happy I had an ocean of tears running down my cheeks. I was laughing and crying all at the same time.

I will never forget that day. We sat down on the grass, and Mum took this beautiful smelling ginger and cream rolled cake from a bag. She also had a big bottle of beautiful Starkey's ginger beer. She had an opener and a glass. I ate the beautiful cake and the tasty drink bubbles went up my nose and had me sneezing. We sat on the lawn talking, eating, drinking and hugging each other so tightly. This was the happiest day of my life. I asked Mum could I keep a piece of the ginger cake so I could give it to Bill later, and Mum wrapped it up for me.

But my joy was not to last long. Mum said she had to go, even though none of the other visitors were going. "I have to go to Havilah to see Neville," she said. Before going she walked me back to the cottage, came in and looked around and saw my bed. I said: "I make my own bed." She said it was beautifully well made. Then she gave me a kiss and a huge hug and left.

The sadness was with me once again. That night I cried myself to sleep.

It was to be one year before I saw Mum again, and even though my brother Neville was only a few hundred yards away in Havilah, I never saw him. It would have been nice if someone had thought to take me over to see him, but that never was to be.

Every Saturday after lunch, I would walk up to the front fence to the entrance gates facing Pennant Hills Road, near the bus stop, where I'd wait and watch everyone else's mums and dads coming and going, looking for Mum's blonde hair which stood out like a beacon. But unfortunately for me, no Mum. Sometimes I would ask myself: "Have I missed her?" There were times when I also wondered about my father and I'd ask myself: "Does he know I'm here and does he care?" I began to hate Saturdays, simply because they only brought me pain and disappointment.

When I was upset I needed seclusion, where other boys couldn't see me crying: I didn't want more tormenting, which made me feel very insecure, so I'd keep my heartache to myself.

Carl Beauchamp

But even though I had been hurt immensely, I still wanted my mother and her love more than anything on this earth.

I think it was while I was at Carlingford that my father began a new relationship with Beryl Chudleigh, who was a school friend of Dad's sister Ruby. Shortly afterwards Dad divorced Mum and married Beryl.

Later that year we learned that we had won the war. It was early morning and all the boys from the Carlingford Home marched up Pennant Hills Road celebrating. Some boys had drums, other boys had tins, and we made as much noise as possible. As we marched we sang the following words to a tune, all in rhythm: "Hitler's dead, he died last night in bed." The same words over and over in repetitive enthusiasm, and as we marched we all made up other words to fit this very special occasion.

3

Home again

Time passed by at the Home. I could hardly remember what my brother Neville looked like, having last seen him leaving Mr Hill's office and walking with Mum out of my sight. I had aged a year and was now eight.

One day I was called by my cottage mother and she walked me hand in hand to Mr Hill's office. There in the office Mr Hill told me I was going home the next day. He said my mother was collecting Neville and me and taking us both home to Erskineville. He did not tell me why my Mum had decided to take me back and to this day I still don't know the answer.

It was strange: I felt so sad to be leaving and yet I was happy to be going home with Mum and as usual when my emotions took over my eyes became oceans of tears. I had grown very fond of Mr Hill and Matron Hill and my kind cottage mother. All three had treated me with so much love and kindness, which has been remembered all my life.

Mr Hill said: "Come on Carl, this is a time for happiness. Now go back to your cottage and pack all your belongings." I went to my room and packed my things, which was everything the Home had given me: clothing and shoes and sandshoes and a jumper and pyjamas and toothbrush and things. I was leaving with so much more than I came with. But the most important thing I left with was the love and kindness of people who really cared about me.

My cottage mother had a tear in her eyes as I said goodbye. It was a sad moment for me. A few of my cottage mates also came over and said goodbye, including Bill who put his hand on my back and said: "See you Carlie."

When my mother turned up, I was shocked to see she had a man with her: her new husband, Stanley Skidmore. Stan and Mum had married at Newtown in 1945. Stan was about 5 feet 8 inches tall with very dark hair, slicked back with oil. He had dark eyes. Mum introduced him but I was in shock, especially when she said he was my new father. For an eight-year-old this was going to take some getting used to. Stan was never called Dad, as we could not accept him as a father.

I did not greet my mother with love or emotion of any kind: no hug, nothing. I believe my love and confidence had been shattered and lost, with no love left to give her, just like Mum had shown us no love. It appeared to me from the time Mum had dumped me at Carlingford that my true love for her was lost and was never to be restored again.

As I walked with Mum from Mr Hill's office, Matron Hill gave me a pat on the head and said goodbye. I kept walking without looking back; little did I realise then that before a year had passed, I'd be wishing I was back here at Carlingford, amongst kind people who truly cared about me.

After leaving Mr Hill's office, we proceeded to Havilah next door, where we picked up Neville. It was good to see him. I did not think I'd remember what he looked like, but I did. We caught the bus to Epping railway station, then onto the train to the City, then another bus to outside our house at 39 Albert Street, Erskineville: the same house I had been removed from one year or so earlier.

LIFE AS A YOUNG BOY IN ERSKINEVILLE

Things were different now, but then again not so different. My father was gone, and in his place was a stepfather who drank beer like a fish, just like Mum. The house and hotel opposite were the same. Slowly everything at the back of my memory began to come back to me as the anaesthetic of being away wore off.

Over time we got used to Stan. In his own way he was a good man. In the first few weeks home, he bought us a little cross collie-kelpie pup, which we called Billy Boy. He was a good dog growing up and very protective of me: God help anyone who tried to lay a hand on me. We also had a ginger cat named Ginger: what else would you call a ginger cat? They were mates.

Soon Neville and I were both attending Erskineville Primary School, and I liked it very much. I was very fond of my teacher: she seemed to care about me, she was kind, and she even gave me the occasional hug. One day she told the class she was leaving. I was downcast and the hurt was tremendous. It seemed that everything I loved, I lost. I was learning that life had many directions, and that life's many changes could be painful.

The other problem was that my sadness was affecting my schoolwork. I was unable to grasp on to things and learn things like most other boys. I felt I was dumb and stupid. I had no self-confidence, was insecure and was always feeling sorry for myself.

The big boys at school worried me. I soon realised I had to stand up for myself. I got into a couple of fist fights with one of the main bullies, not knowing that by standing up to him I would soon be thought of differently by the other bullies. They learnt that I was not one to be messed with. They could not believe a quiet little kid like me had so much courage and tenacity. It finished with the bully giving up, and at last I was respected.

Most of the boys at school now became my friends, with no-one picking on me or tormenting me anymore. It appeared the bully who I fought into submission was regarded as the school's top fighter. To me he was just a bully picking on small kids who he thought were easy to hurt. I was now the David who overcame Goliath as the Bible story tells us: little Carlie now being treated with respect and an equal. Now all the kids were allowing me to play in their games and when picking teams, they all wanted me. This helped me over time get some self-confidence back. But I did not allow myself to be part of any special group, and still played mostly with my softer mates. If I saw a bully picking on any of my softer mates, all I had to do was tell them to leave them alone and they stopped.

Soon I was involved in every sport. I loved cricket and rugby league, where I played in the school five stone sevens competition. Even if I say so myself, I was good at sport. Soon I was in for a shock: I was one of the first chosen in the five stone seven pound District League Competition. While playing in the District School Football Competition I stood out. I had no boots, so I played in a pair loaned to me by the teacher. His name was Mr Feeney. He was a very good but very strict teacher. Nobody messed with Mr Feeney.

My school team was called the Kangaroos, and one day whilst playing interschool football and enjoying a good game, unbeknown to me the selectors were watching. They chose me to play in a trial match for the School State Football competition. I was very happy, and I told my Mum that night what the selectors had said: that I had to have a good pair of footy boots. But she refused to buy them. I told the sports master who was as disappointed as I was: I could no longer wear the on-loan boots because the teacher had returned them to the owner.

I continued to play footy for the school and in made-up teams on sports days, without boots, but if I wanted to be part of a representative team I had to have boots. Sport was all I had; it was the best part of my life. Schoolwork like spelling, arithmetic and geography was a bore, mainly because I could not concentrate: I felt like I had no brains. I found I could not comprehend how arithmetic worked. One thing for sure: I was only good at sport.

Most days after school I would get down to the park with my mates and play footy up until about five o'clock, knowing Mum would soon be home. I played bare-footed and if we had no ball we would use rolled-up clothing as a substitute. Sometimes after playing we would grab a drink at the Milk Bar. Ivan Grant, David DeBelin or Kenny Penning would put in a share to buy me a drink because I never had any money. Sometimes Barry Chapman would put in also. They were the best mates one could ever have, everyone sharing. Even the girls shared and often they would play footy with us to make up the teams.

Maybe I should talk a bit about what life was like for us poorer kids at that time. Only rich families had an old Silent Knight refrigerator. Most families only had an "ice box" which kept food cool by the use of a large square block of ice which was delivered from the horse and cart to inside your ice box. The ice cost about sixpence. Under the ice box was a drip tray that had to be emptied twice a day. Should you forget – and we often forgot to empty the tray – there would be water all over and under the lino, which soon rotted the lino.

I don't recall anybody having a "washing machine". All our clothing was boiled in a copper, which was filled with cold water and heated up by a wood fire below. Mum had a three-foot long wooden stick, which she used to pick the hot clothes out into a nearby tub. The heated water would later be taken from the copper in a tin bucket and carried into the galvanised tin bath for all of us to bathe in. Then the copper would be refilled with clean cold water for the next lot of clothing to be washed. So washing day was also our once a week bath in the old galvanised tin bath. We had no fancy smelling fragrant soap: we had to use a clothes washing soap called Life Buoy.

The clothes in the tub would be rinsed then wrung out by hand, getting as much water out as possible. I would wring one end of a garment, wringing to my right, and Mum would do likewise at the other end. A few of the neighbours had a hand wringer, which was screwed to the side of the concrete tubs. This had a handle which you turned as you pushed the clothing through the rubber rollers. If the clothing was real dirty, Mum had to rub the soaped items on a corrugated washing board over and over until they looked reasonable.

The clothes were then hung on the line with wooden pegs and the clothesline would be raised high by a wooden prop from the centre of the line.

Once a week a man would push his wooden trolley down our street, calling out "soap and disinfectant". Mum would bring her own bottle out to be filled up for sixpence. He also sold bars of washing soap, which had a caustic soda smell, and he also sold kerosene. Sometimes he had a horse and cart and had stacks of long wooden props, which cost one shilling. We used these for pushing the clothesline up to get the wind.

Also once a week a man on his horse and cart would come around the streets of Erskineville selling rabbits, sometimes still with the fur still attached, sometimes already skinned. These sold for between sixpence and a shilling depending on size and how many he had for sale. Sometimes we would eat them baked with seasoned herb stuffing; other times they became rabbit stew and if there was any curry in the house we had curried rabbit. Any left over would be used for sandwich lunches. We did not have any of these very often, simply because Mum mostly could not be bothered cooking. But when Ma Kate Morris lived with us, we enjoyed these simple luxuries more often because Ma cared about us and knew Mum was not looking after us. Ma was an altruistic, smart lady who loved us deeply. Ma Morris taught me to read my first book, which was the Bible. Her favourites were Proverbs and Revelations.

When the horses passed by our house they often left a trail of manure. If I saw it I would rush around to get an old sack and a spade and pick it all up. It was good for my little garden that I had in the backyard. If I had too much I would sell it to an old lady in Burren Street who also bought wood from me for her stove. I believe she took pity on my brother and me: she was very kind. She often had a little piece of cake put aside on a plate for us.

The milkman who had a horse and cart with many silver containers delivered the milk, cream and butter. He would go from house to house pouring from these into the milk-jugs or milk-cans left out near the front door with the correct money and a note requesting how much milk they wanted. Most people took a pint whilst others took a quart. I cannot ever recall Mum buying cream or butter, probably because she could not afford such luxuries. Beer was much cheaper.

In those days everybody cooked by either a wood or coal stove, or, if they had a gas meter, using gas. You paid by putting a penny or two into the meter. When the money ran out you put another penny in the meter box. The gas in those days had a very strong smell and was deadly if you left the stove on unlit. Because of people being careless there were often deaths, which I once witnessed in Albert Street when the authorities removed dead bodies from the house.

In the early days in these houses in Albert Street there were gaslights coming out of the wall in each room. They were lit by match and gave a little light. Most people preferred to use candles that were safer as long as you were careful. You made sure you kept them away from curtains or inflammable things. Mum had matches that were made of wax in a small round box, which you struck on the bottom to light. These matches could be dangerous and if rats got to them they could be easily ignited and cause a fire.

Toilet paper was only for the rich: the rest of us used newspaper, which was cut up in squares, and these would be placed on hooks in the toilet. You had to be very careful that you did not use too much for fear of blocking the sewer pipes. These pipes often blocked and would build up and overflow your toilet bowl. Often Mum would have Neville and me pushing a long piece of strong wire down the toilet pipe to clear the blockage and after that clean up the filthy foul smelling mess and carry it to a hole we dug in the backyard. Mum never helped us.

In today's world most people have a telephone, but in my younger days very few people had a phone in their homes. If by luck you did have a phone it was often linked up where two homes shared the same line and number. The phone would ring and often both shared lines would pick up and whomever the call was for would stay on line. If the neighbours were on a share line speaking, you had no alternative but to wait until they hung up. I know this worked OK because Ma and Pa Beauchamp shared such a line with the neighbouring milk carter next door in Dulwich Hill.

The only places that had the phone connection in my street in Erskineville were the Cosmopolitan Hotel and the corner grocer. If we ever needed to use the phone there was only the one at the phone box attached to the Erskineville Post Office on Erskineville Road. A few shops in other nearby streets also had the phone on, as did the other local hotels. The public phone often had a queue of people waiting to use it. If the users took too long, those waiting would hurry them up by tapping on the glass

Come home, you little bastards

door. Often things turned nasty with abuse and the occasional fight. We loved watching people bash each other up: sometimes the men had coins falling from their pockets onto the street, and we were very quick to pick up the coins, which made our day.

Not every family had a wireless. We had an old His Masters Voice, which was our only entertainment, and we loved listening to the afternoon serials, but my mother soon put a stop to this. One day during a drunken brawl with her second husband Stan she threw it at him, missed and hit the wall. It was broken into a thousand pieces. It was years before we got another one. This was our only entertainment and we missed our regular evening programs.

Earlier I said that in our street we had a man pushing a handcart filled with disinfectant. He knocked on the doors of all his customers. This poor chap could not read or write. He also had a speech impediment and his clothes were all worn out with holes. The lady next door felt sorry for him and without fail each week she had a drink ready for him. Everyone brought out the usual containers and he would fill them with his various mixtures, phenyl, eucalyptus disinfectant etc.

Another man selling firewood and coal and coke laden to the hilt on his cart always stopped outside our house. He would ask us to watch his load whilst he ran across to Mrs Hartigan's Cosmopolitan Hotel for a beer or two. On his return he would always check his load then give us a few pennies for our services. One Christmas he gave Mum a free bag of firewood and gave Neville and me sixpence each. He was poor like us but he had a kind heart.

In those days soft drink was sometimes delivered by "Sharpies". The drink was in stoneware jugs, which held about one gallon. Most flavours were available. Mum bought a jar now and then, but it had to be a special occasion for her to buy drinks for us. Her favourites were Ginger Ale and Ginger Beer. The most popular brands in the shops were Marchant's, Shelley's and Starkey's, but there were others like Coke and Pepsi and Canadian Dry.

Mum never ironed my brothers or my clothes, probably because they were not worth ironing! She always took special care with her clothing to make sure the iron, which was heated up on the gas stove, did not damage her clothes. She mixed her own starch and if she had a lemon she would squeeze the lemon juice into the starch water.

Mum used to smoke Craven A and Capstan cigarettes. If she was particularly short of money she would smoke the old cheapies, Old Chums or Woodbine, which were less than half the price of the good brands.

THE SAME OLD PROBLEMS AGAIN

Drinking parties and wild sex orgies became a regular thing again at our house, with zombie looking drunks walking through our house, even into our bedroom, falling asleep on our beds and leaving Neville and me with no bed to sleep on. One day I poured a glass of water over the drunk in my bed. He jumped up swearing and fell over headfirst, because I had tied his shoelaces together. His profane language woke the rest of the drunks up.

After all the sex-crazed drunks had left, Mum always had Neville and me clean up the mess. Often we would find money that had fallen from their clothes, which we salvaged as our small reward: we would keep it to buy ourselves lollies and Pepsi or whatever.

As time passed, the good clothing given to us from the Carlingford Church of England Boys' Home was becoming threadbare. Mum showed no interest in anything we did at school or in our clothes being worn out. I was now past my ninth birthday and as usual had received no gifts. I had no shoes, what I had was long worn out, my pants were full of holes and it was embarrassing.

Eventually because of embarrassment about my clothes and no shoes and having no confidence to learn at school, I started to wag school. The only thing I missed from school was our free bottle of milk each playtime, which most days was all we had to sustain us.

We knew that if we were to survive we had to adopt an independent mind set, beholden to nobody, and if it meant stealing from our neighbours, so be it. It was obvious to our immediate neighbours that we were neglected and often unfed. But did they ever offer us any help, like food or drink? No they did not, but they did report us to Child Welfare after noticing that their milk money and clothing from their lines were disappearing on a regular basis.

Life at home had reached a stage where Mum often went missing for days, even up to a full week, and then all of a sudden she would reappear as if nothing had happened. She would stay with her men friends and Stan did not appear all that concerned: he would just run off to his mother's for days at a time. She lived only two blocks from us, in Septimus Street. Stan was drinking very heavily and betting a lot with the SP bookies. Tommy Hartigan once said to us: "I'm always willing to take a mug's money."

Mum just was not concerned for us. She knew there was no food in the house. Even if we had food to cook, we still needed money to put in the gas meter.

The Child Welfare truant inspectors had been coming and door knocking, but we would sneak a look out the window and realise who they were and would not answer the door. They left notes for Mum, which we would never give her: we just ripped the notes up and threw them away.

One Saturday I walked into the kitchen downstairs. Sometimes Mum would allow us to go to the afternoon pictures at the Hoyts or the Hub at Newtown or the Hub number 2 on Erskineville Road. Well this afternoon Mum had promised we could go and she was going to give us a shilling each, but we were not to be so lucky. Before we could go, we had to place some bets and then go and buy two bottles of wine. The pub was closed as it was Saturday afternoon, but you could still buy grog illegally from the 'sly grog' house in Charles Street owned by Mr Cleary, who had a new Standard car.

So here I am standing at the kitchen table and Stan and Mum, who had both been drinking heavily, are seated giving me instructions. Stan or my mother, can't remember which, was waving a large sharp bread knife around near my right hand, hitting it a few times with the blunt end, trying to make their point. The knife slipped and turned and next thing my hand had this deep gash across it. I thought my hand would fall off, the cut looked so bad to me. Mum rushed me outside to the street; here she stopped a man driving past, who took me to Prince Alfred Hospital. Mum did not know the driver and Mum did not come with me: instead she went back inside to her drinking.

The doctors saw me straight away because my hand looked a mess. They got to work pulling the skin together with horsehair and then cutting off after each stitch. They did this about 15 times and it hurt. For years after the pain was still there. After they placed a bandage on my hand they allowed me to go home by myself. I walked home and went inside, but neither Mum nor Stan bothered to ask how I was or even look at my hand: they both were so drunk. Our promised afternoon at the pictures became just a dream, just another broken promise, which was very normal for Mum.

The following week I returned alone to the hospital, because

Come home, you little bastards

they had to remove the stitches. It was during this period that I pledged if ever I became a father I'd treat my kids much better.

As my hand healed, Mum must have felt sorry for us, because she walked us up to Newtown to be taught acrobatics and tap dancing. I didn't go much on tap dancing, but I loved the acrobatics. Mum's sister Lydia – we called her Aunty Bub – had our cousin Kathleen there learning both acrobatics and dancing. When we saw Kathleen doing her thing we were delighted to see how good she was. Because of my badly cut hand becoming very weak, my wrists were strapped to withstand the stress of the acrobatic lessons.

We were enjoying our twice-weekly lessons, but shortly after Mum decided that she could no longer afford it and promptly ceased our lessons. I had met a girl my own age there. Her name was Pam Harrison, my first girlfriend albeit only for a few months. She cried when I told her I could not come to lessons again and then I cried all the way home.

Christmas was drawing near and Stan received a very good holiday bonus. I was only 10 and seeing all these large denomination banknotes for the first time ever had me intrigued. I asked Stan could I hold one, which he let me do for a few moments. Saturday came and Stan was up early and went by bus into the City. Later in the day he came home with two new beautiful suits, which had been made by the tailors in town at Broadway, near Central Railway Station.

Stan left the suits on the double bed in the upstairs front room. I think they planned to go out to a party, but something happened and Mum and Stan had a big fight. Stan raced out the front door and stormed over to the Cosmopolitan Hotel, where he stayed a few hours drinking with his inebriated mates and enjoying himself.

In an agitated state of mind, Mum was waiting at home for his return. She heard the key turning in the door lock but it would not open, because she had bolted the indoor lock. Mum raced upstairs to the top front bedroom and out onto the top verandah with his two new suits. Mum was waving the scissors around with his new suits draped over the verandah rail. Stan was below on the footpath yelling to be let in. All the neighbours were out to watch the entertainment as Mum started cutting little pieces from his suits, small pieces becoming larger pieces and falling to the ground. Stan just stood there like a stunned mullet, watching helplessly as piece after piece of his new unworn suits floated to the footpath.

Mum was in her delight as Stan called her a hare-brained trollop and a vile slut mixed with every conceivable swear word. Mum, angered by his abuse and not to be outdone by Stan, yelled out loudly that Stan was worthless in bed and had such a small cock that she never received any satisfaction. Blokes from outside the hotel yelled out to Mum: "Tell us: how small is Stan's cock?" Mum shouted back that his penis was so small you needed a microscope to see it. With this all of his mates outside the hotel started laughing loudly, to Stan's embarrassment. Stan retaliated by calling her a whore and a dead root, and said she had a smelly fanny and that he had inherited sexual sores from her.

Mum got much enjoyment seeing Stan's reaction to the suit cutting and also enjoyed giving the neighbours and hotel drunks a laugh at Stan's expense. Stan screamed out: "I'll kill you when I get you." But Mum knew she had his measure. She went downstairs and unbolted the door, which she stepped behind; as he rushed in he turned around facing Mum, who hit him over the head with a full bottle of plonk. His skull was split wide open, with streams of blood squirting over the walls. As he fell to the ground, Mum continued hitting him around the head with the full bottle of plonk. Mum yelled out: "Cop this you little prick. I'll teach you to make fun out of me with your poofter mates."

I recall Mum was like a mad woman. She frightened me, so I

ran outside to the Hotel and asked for the police to be called and an ambulance because I thought she might have killed Stan. But Stan was not dead: staggering, he headed for his mother's house two blocks away.

Mum grabbed our hands and dragged us along, chasing after Stan. On catching up with Stan, who by that stage was being comforted by his mother and sisters who were trying to wrap up the head wound, Mum like a mad woman tore into his sisters Joyce and Mavis. The fight continued in the middle of the street, with Mum punching the two sisters and pulling out handful after handful of hair.

The police eventually arrived, by which stage Mum had quietened down. They pushed Mum into the Black Maria and spoke to the victims. All told their stories and then the police, knowing we were her kids, put us in the front seat and drove us to Newtown Police Station. What the outcome was, I never found out. Within a few days, Mum and Stan were living together again.

But Mum and Stan's peace treaty was not longlasting. It was a Friday night and the usual sex party was taking place. Stan was drunk and out of this world. For one reason or another, Neville and I crept down the stairs. Stan was asleep on the floor and the place was a mess. We could not see Mum. We proceeded to walk back up the stairs. We heard groaning sounds, and turning around over on the settee we could see Mum in the act of sexual intercourse with a man we could not see properly. Mum was on top and moving up and down very fast, groaning louder and louder.

We tried not to be noticed and kept going up the stairs, which squeaked, drawing Mum's attention to us. Mum jumped off the man in the nude, and called us everything she could think of. We raced to our room and bolted the door. We were frightened she might break in to hit us, so we jumped out the window and onto the roof below, then down onto the next level. We lowered ourselves to the ground. We had often done this before, to sneak out to hang out with our mates under the lights in Charles Street. This night we just hid ourselves in the back yard laundry where, cold and shivering, she found us asleep the next morning. She was still in the nude and hit both of us over the head with the copper stick. She then dragged us inside and made us clean up the mess in the house. Her boyfriend was still lying there asleep with no clothes on, and we cleaned up around him.

About this time, when I was between nine and ten years, our father called in to see us. Reg was making a visit to see Mum while Stan was at work. They retreated up to Mum's top front bedroom for a few hours. That was around 1947. I had not seen him for a few years.

Reg was given permission to take us for weekends every now and then. A few times we were taken for a week or two for a holiday with Reg's new family, often to Forster, a town on the coast north of Sydney. Neville and I looked forward to these holidays. It was so nice with everyone enjoying each other's company.

Reg and Beryl, his new wife, with the help of Seth and Fred, Reg's brothers, had built a little weekender at Forster and they had a motorboat. We used to enjoy our days out on the water fishing, and it gave us a chance to know each other better. But like all good things the happiness had to end and we returned home to Mum's den of iniquity. Often we would have a few new comics Reg had bought us, which we treasured, and would bring home fresh fish and crabs we had helped catch. The blue swimmer crabs were very big: as wide as the top of a bucket. Mum sometimes accepted these in a grateful manner. Other times if we arrived home late or if she was in one of her drunken, aggressive moods, anything could happen.

One Sunday we had paid a short visit to Reg's parents at their new Oatley home. Pa and Reg and Neville and I had gone out in Pa's boat fishing on Georges River. While out fishing with Pa nobody ever spoke: everything was sign language. Silence was the key to good fishing, Pa often said.

While out fishing I caught my first flathead. It was a beauty. I did not even know it was on my line until I had it near pulled in. Pa with his smoke to the side of his mouth saw it first. He assisted me in bringing it in. He placed the net in the water under the flathead and gave it no chance of escape. I was overjoyed and so pleased with myself. These outings with Pa and Reg helped me regain confidence in myself.

After the fishing was finished, we all got stuck into cleaning and scaling the fish on the rocks near Pa's jetty. Normally we would come into the house and Pa would call out to Ma: "Fresh fish tonight," and Ma would prepare the fish for cooking. Later we would all sit around the meal table and eat fresh cooked fish: the smell was so beautiful.

But I did not want my flathead eaten, so Pa had placed it aside for me to take home to show my Mum how good I was at fishing. During the afternoon whilst we were out fishing, Beryl had cooked a sponge cake and filled it with cream and jam. Beryl made the best cakes ever. Our own mother had no idea how to cook cakes. Often these sponges were made for us to take home. Beryl knew Neville and I appreciated it. She also knew that we never saw any cakes at home with Mum.

Reg and Beryl drove us home as usual. I used to hope the trips home would take a long time; I was never in any rush to get home. But sadly we were soon home parked outside 39 Albert Street. None of us rushed to get out of the car, which was a black Buick with a beautiful smelling leather interior.

Reg knocked and knocked on our front door. Eventually Mum opened the door, swearing at Reg for being late. Reg said: "You're drunk again." Mum said she was not drunk and only had a headache. Looking at us she then said: "So you decided to come home you little bastards?" and then: "Why did you bother?"

One angry malicious word led to another. She could see Reg was tired and in no mood to argue. Reg said: "I'd love to keep them both. Can we?" Then Beryl called from the car: "Bebe, if you don't want them, we would be only too pleased to have them. Will you get what little clothing they have and then we'll be off."

Mum soon realised her angry words had backfired, as Reg said to her: "If we keep the kids, your weekly maintenance of thirty shillings a fortnight will cease." This fired her up to the point of exploding, telling us: "Come in here you bloody bastards, you will not be going out with your ****** father again or ****** bloody Beryl." Mum then spotted the sponge cake Beryl had made for us. Mum grabbed it from my hands and in one movement smashed the cake into my father's face, then went to the car and wiped the cream on her hands over Beryl's hair.

By this time Beryl was screaming out to Reg: "Come to the car and let's get out of here!" But Reg was not going to leave us in this situation. By this time, Mum had grabbed my bag of fish, some falling to the footpath. Mum picked up my big flathead and threw it into Beryl's face from a short distance. While this was going on, Reg grabbed Neville and me and bundled us into the rear seat of the car. Reg then started the car and proceeded to drive off, with Mum clinging to the car door and screaming every foul word you could think of and then some more, inventing them as she raged on.

Reg drove us to his place. On arriving home he proceeded to make a few phone calls, but first he had to wait until the neighbours next door who they shared a line with had hung up. Whoever Reg spoke to we do not know: he never told us. Beryl took us to the bathroom and ran a nice hot bath for us. Beryl then got us some clothing for bed. It was not long before we were asleep.

Next morning we had breakfast and Reg then took us home. On reaching home, Reg had a few words with Mum, a little angst but no fighting. Then they went up to Mum's bedroom and were up there together for a long time. They both came down and were hugging each other. Then Reg departed. We did not go to school that day.

A few weeks later, Mum and Stan had another vicious fight, which started in Albert Street and worked its way to Stan's mother's house in Septimus Street. Neighbours with their children followed the fight, urging Stan to hit Mum, saying "hit the bitch" and other things not very pleasant. As they got to the Skidmore house, old Mrs Skidmore appeared out the front. Mum abused the hell out of her. Mum picked up a house brick and threw it through the front window, then laid into poor old Mrs Skidmore.

Mum knocked her to the ground and Neville and I tried our hardest to pull Mum off her, but she was too strong and we couldn't get her off. We stood in the centre of Septimus Street, scared and crying as Mum continued her madness. Stan's sisters had come to their Mum's aid. They tried to talk sense to Mum, but she would not listen to their pleas. Where was Stan while all this mayhem was taking place? He had collapsed through exhaustion from fighting and being so drunk.

Someone had called the police from Newtown, which was only minutes away. A police bike and sidecar and a Black Maria drove up and parked with four big police officers settling things down and dispersing all the crowd. As they threw Stan into the rear of the police vehicle, the crowd were singing out: "Leave him alone: he did nothing." Mum had already been put into the Maria before Stan. So as to keep them separated, a large policeman got in between them.

Later Stan's mother and two sisters walked up to Newtown Police Station with the intent to lay assault charges against Mum. I know Mum had to go to Court over this nasty business, but what the result was I never found out.

Shortly after this fight, Stan moved out and commenced action to divorce Mum. I often would see Stan sitting outside the Erskineville Post Office. In the square in front of the building were tables and seats. Here men would meet to chat and smoke and drink and spend time playing draughts and card games. No doubt Stan's main topic would be about being to hell and back, having lived with the most selfish lazy bitch who ever lived.

Stan Skidmore was now gone, and my Mum's mother came to live with us. She took our bedroom on the top floor at the back facing Charles Street. Prior to Ma moving in the house had been fumigated, killing off all the dirty bugs and fleas that infested the house. Our blankets and mattresses had all been burnt, so Ma bought new bedding and helped clean up the house.

While Ma was living with us, meals were cooked on a regular basis and everything was much better. Having Ma with us made all the difference to our standard of living.

Sadly 'the good life' was to be short lived. After a year or so, Ma could not take any more of Mum's facetious, snide remarks, which were very hurtful. Mum was back to her old selfish ways, fighting over a variety of things. Mum was not getting home from work until really late. On a weekend she restarted having her many boyfriends and girlfriends in for drinks and sex.

Eventually Ma could take no more and moved to a flat with a woman friend above a toyshop on King Street, Newtown. Neville and I often paid Ma a visit; she would make us really welcome, making us a pot of tea with toast cut into fingers.

It was during these visits to the flat that I grew very fond of Ma, and I think she was as delighted with my visits as I was fond of visiting her. Ma called me her Carlie, probably because that was what she had called her only son who had been killed in 1935. In fact the real reason I visited Ma besides the obvious was to get away from my mother. I did not have the courage to tell Mum of my visits to Ma, because she had warned me not to visit her or have anything to do with Ma. One thing about Ma was she never ran Mum down to us or to anyone else. Ma Kate Morris did not carry hatred and was a very forgiving Catholic.

Mum and my grandmother continued not to talk. Mum knew that preventing Ma seeing us would hurt her. Mother has always been a person who could never find it in herself to apologise or even attempt to work things out: a very stubborn and selfish person was our mother.

When Ma left, she took with her all her bedding, leaving only the old army wire bed. Neville and I had shared a lounge to sleep on when Ma was there, so with delight we moved back into our old room. With only a wire bed and with no bedding, we slept on old newspapers on top of the wire for a long time, until Mum bought another bed and two mattresses from St Vincent de Paul's secondhand store in Newtown, and two pillows, but no sheets.

4

Mates, girls and games

It was just after Christmas in 1949. I was 12 years old, and my mother was still working and getting back home late every evening. The school holidays were about six weeks long and often we were bored and would wander the streets all around the neighbouring suburbs, exploring everything. Sometimes, we would walk all the way to Coogee beach for a swim in the surf, then collect drink bottles and return them to the shops for the deposit money.

My best mates were Ken Penning, Ivan Grant, Davey DeBelin and Barry Chapman, whose nickname was Chicka. Davey had great olive skin. His mother's parents had originally come from Mauritius. Ivan had Aboriginal blood. His ancestors were originally from out west working on the John Grant Estate. John Grant had previously been a convict working for Doctor Redfern who had received many early grants of land from the government.

But colour with us was never thought of, never an issue. I cannot ever recall any racism as I grew up. All my best mates lived in Charles Street. There were a few girl friends too, although we were all mates rather than boyfriends or girlfriends. Ann DeBelin, Daphne Hawkins and a few others whose names I can't remember. Harold DeBelin also used to hang around and his younger sisters, Lola and Daphne.

One of my first girlfriends was a very pretty girl a few years younger than I was. Joan was shy and never said anything that would hurt others. She had blossomed into a mature girl and I found it easy to talk to her. Proudly I referred to Joan as my best girlfriend. She was just one of the gang and did everything we did and if it was a hot day would ask her mother if she could walk to Coogee Beach with us and on occasions she was allowed. With no money we walked, having the time of our lives. We shared our towels: if I recall correctly only the DeBelins and Ivan Grant and Barry Chapman had towels, but they were happy for the rest of us to share theirs.

On hot balmy nights we would often walk around the streets and sometimes sit on the seats in the park at the top of Charles Street, just hanging out and enjoying each other's company. If any of us had money we would put it all together and buy a coke each or share one as we watched people coming and going. Later we would sit under the light of the telegraph pole on the footpath, talking, and sometimes we would sing a few songs together, not that any of us had great singing voices. Al Jolson songs were very popular in those days, especially after the movie *The Jolson Story* was shown at the Hoyts Theatre in Newtown. I remember the line each night to get in went right down to past the Post Office.

On these hot nights, none of us wanted to go home, but eventually as it got late a procession of parents would come to the door, calling out to their respective children: "Time to come home!" Very soon our gang would dwindle to only a few. I was always the last to go home: after all, I had nothing much to go home to, what with only fleas and bugs waiting for me and Mum drunk and always ready to belt us over the head with whatever was nearest.

Rainy days were a great delight for us kids: the heavier the rain the better we liked it. We had a game of racing our ice cream sticks through the torrents of the gutters. We used to paint the sticks and write the names of our favourite racehorses on them. We would race up and down the gutter for hours. My ice cream stick horse was named Flight. Flight was a mare bought for next to nothing by a Mr Crowley who was on the AJC committee, Flight once beat the champion horse Bernborough, and made Mr Crowley a small fortune.

We would all have a go at being Ken Howard, the famous horse race caller. Davey always called his ice cream stick Bernborough, and Ivan had Russia and Ken had San Dominico. I recall Barry Chapman used various names, but I always stuck with Flight, my favourite. We enjoyed our gutter racing; it was simple and didn't cost anything.

Some days we would congregate on the verandah of one of our homes. We would sit around and play cards or play car games. Each of us would guess say how many Fords, Dodges or Buicks would come past us in the hour, or what cars would have the same colour.

During the winter weekdays, my mates and I would often visit Erskineville Oval and play footy on the grass outside the Oval. On the winter nights, the Newtown Bluebags rugby league team would train, beginning at five o'clock. Uninvited, we would train with them, running around the oval. My favourite player was Keith Froome and I ran near him, but steered clear of Frank "Bumper" Farrell who was a well-known policeman. He often told us to "piss off." Big Mick Carter had bright red hair and owned a fruit shop on Erskineville Road. He trained harder than most. Jack Troy was a very fast winger and there was Jack

Carl Beauchamp

Debenham, the fullback who later went to Wests. These were great days rubbing shoulder to shoulder with our favourite team. They were unforgettable moments in our young lives.

One day about 12 of us were up at the Wilson Street Park, having fun playing on the swings and slippery dips and the roundabout. There was another local group hanging out. We took no notice of them until one bully pushed Ann DeBelin off the swing. We did nothing because Ann did not appear worried. Later they moved on and we had the park to ourselves.

After a while we started heading for home, and as we walked down the lane off Wilson Street we were ambushed by the Wilson Street gang, which had grown to about 20. They started throwing rocks of all sizes at us, so we ran out of their throwing range.

I think they thought they had frightened us off and started walking towards us, throwing rocks again. But we had collected as many rocks as we could carry in our pockets, so we retaliated big time, like William Wallace of *Braveheart* fame. We threw our rocks all at once and they poured from the sky to find the target. With us on the attack they retreated and immediately we charged. One of our rocks hit one of them on the head and he fell to the ground. Blood was pouring out of the wound. It was a big gash and looked bad. All his so-called mates ran off, leaving him at our mercy. We were trying to wrap his shirt around his head and talk to him, asking why they had attacked us. Before he answered we noticed a few adults coming from the back lane gates of the double storey terrace houses, so we took off for home. We saw the boy a week later at the park with his head still bandaged.

As we grew up, us boys began to notice that girls were different and we treated them less roughly. From an early age we began to hold hands and even steal a kiss here and there. From here we all started to experiment in sex, just touching each other at first and later doing more, but it was not real penetrating sex: we were just beginning to teach ourselves about the 'birds and the bees'. Neville and I knew all about sex because we often saw Mum having it off with numerous boyfriends.

We would touch each other in places we never thought of before. This only happened when we knew we had the house to ourselves. Looking back I can see how funny we must have been, young kids learning all about sex by ourselves. None of us had any education about this wonderful phenomenon that was suddenly thrust upon us. The fact that some of my mates and I had previously seen sex orgies of Mum and her friends had us very eager to learn more. The strange thing is, I cannot ever recall the Minister at church warning us that God never meant this for young people like us and meant it only for married people. In those days even Ministers did not speak of sex in church, or if they did it was so obtuse that I never understood.

FOOD AND CLOTHES

Things were becoming difficult once more at home, with no regular meals. But we did not want to be put into a Boys' Home again, so we did our best not to create trouble or problems near home. Quite often we would have a meal at my friend Dave DeBelin's home, Davey asking his mother Mrs DeBelin: "Could the Beauchamp kids have lunch with us?" Very rarely did she say no. She did not like to refuse, knowing our circumstances.

Mr and Mrs DeBelin liked a drink here and there, but unlike our Mum they knew when they had had enough. They never neglected their children, who always came first. Mrs DeBelin had words with Mum at the Erskineville Hotel once, and they did not like each other. The DeBelins were very good Catholics, with the children going to Catholic schools, which many people believed led to a better education.

On a Sunday in Erskineville, you would walk down the streets near my street and smell the baked Sunday dinners where everyone either had legs of lamb or a beef roast and beautiful baked vegetables. Being poor did not prevent most families having the once-a-week baked Sunday dinner, because meat was relatively cheap then. Ours was one of the few families that rarely had Sunday dinner. Neville and I grew up living on bread and dripping. Sometimes we would have fried bread, today known as French toast.

On Sundays we would try and be around one of my mates' houses on their front verandahs around lunchtime. Most times we would get an invitation from the DeBelins or the Chapmans or the Grants – all three families knew about the Beauchamps living in harsh conditions and took pity on us.

One day Mum had this shopping expedition so she could dress up for a night out. Later in the afternoon she was ready, dressed to the nines. She looked so beautiful, like one of those good-looking movie stars. That evening when she went out wearing her new fluffy coat, she said she might not be home for a few days. It must have been some party, because Mum didn't come home for a week. Neville and I coped with this many times. Of course there was no food in the house, but we did have one gallon of Sharps Ginger Ale to drink all to ourselves.

With Mum gone and no food in the house, somehow we had to survive. We were hungry and cold and for the first time in my life, just before she left, I stole money from her purse, which she had left on the table whilst she went to the toilet down the back yard near the rear gate. I think it was about four shillings. I hid it under the lino as she came in. I must have looked guilty, but she was in too much of a hurry to notice as she rushed off. I was already upset with Mum because we both badly needed pants: our only pants were full of holes.

The next morning we got out of bed, looked around, Mum

was not home, so we went to the kitchen cupboard and there was only bread and some dripping in the baking dish and some salt and sugar and a few cereal biscuits. So I took the four shillings from under the lino and went to the corner shop two buildings away. I bought three pence of Devon sausage, went home and Neville and I had a Devon on dry bread sandwich each, leaving enough bread for dripping sandwiches later.

On the Monday, Neville and I went up to the St Vinnies second hand shop near the St George's Hall building in Newtown. Neville and I strolled into St Vinnies and spent a long time sifting through a myriad of old clothing with the very distinctive smell old second hand clothes have. As we found suitable clothes we placed them aside, then we went to the shoe table and picked out two old pairs of sandshoes. To most people they were rubbish, but for us they were beautiful. We tried them on our feet and we were happy with the fit. We also chose a woollen jumper each.

I fronted up to the old lady at the counter and showed her what we had and she added up the cost on a piece of paper and told us the cost was four shillings and sixpence. I only had three shillings and ninepence. I was nine pence short. I became upset, which she noticed. Taking pity on us she said: "Take it all and pay me the ninepence next time you're up here." I don't remember ever paying the ninepence back, forgetting all about it as kids do.

Talking about old clothing, about a year prior to going to St Vinnies our pants had been more holes than cloth. In fact they were rags and beyond repair. One late afternoon I saw Mrs Hardman and Mrs Williams hanging the washing on their clotheslines, then extending the lines high with the clothes prop. Later I noticed both these ladies out the front talking to Mrs Humphries and Jack Crimmins. I had Neville act as 'cockatoo' to warn me if they went inside their houses. I rushed down the back and jumped the fence and stole a pair of men's trousers from Mrs Hardman's clothesline.

Back home I found a pair of Mum's scissors. I cut the long trousers down to a size to fit me, with some rope for the waist I used as a belt. With the off-cuts we got Mum's sewing needle and cotton and sewed them on Neville's holey pants, covering all the holes. I reckon Mrs Hardman recognised what we were wearing were her husband's pants, because she would often stare at us. I was glad nothing was ever said. It was probably because Mum had had blues many times with them and they were frightened of her and her temper.

But they did manage to square the score, as they made many complaints to the Child Welfare about us, with the result being visits to our place by the Child Welfare. They were persistent, coming back time after time, but we refused to open the door as we guessed who they were: we did not want to be taken away again. After they left, we would reappear on the street to play games. I think we were always one step in front of these mongrels trying to nab us neglected kids.

Because of Mum's working hours, they could never catch her at home. We were quite smart knowing they would send letters to Mum, and indeed they did. I'd open the letters by steam and read them and if they were from the Welfare they were immediately burnt. I became very good at spotting Child Welfare inspectors, because of the way they dressed differently from ordinary folk. But our luck could not last and eventually they contacted Mum.

Going back to that week when Mum was away enjoying herself, we were soon near starving again once the bread had been consumed. I realised I had to take drastic action. So one morning very early after the milkman had made his deliveries, I took our empty milk jug and another container containing water. I went to a nearby house and from their full jug of milk poured about a third into my jug. I then added water to their milk jug, right up to the top. My thinking was they would not notice the milk had been watered down.

I did the same to one or two other houses then went home, hoping nobody had seen me. If the milkman had left a little change, I put it in my pocket. The money I lifted was only enough to buy a loaf of bread. When the baker came later in the day, I went over as he opened the door of the cart. The beautiful aroma of the fresh bread was overwhelming, making me so hungry I wanted to eat it immediately. I could not wait to get inside to put some dripping on it. Unless you have experienced the beautiful taste and aroma of newly baked bread back in those years, you've missed a great treat: bread today is so tasteless and has no aroma. Believe me, I know what I'm saying, having worked in today's modern bakeries for 14 years.

After having a slice of bread, I grabbed an old wheat bag and went outside to where the baker's horse had left a pile of manure. I shovelled it up with my hands into the bag to later use on my little garden.

Well, the following week when Mum came home, she noticed our pants and sandshoes and jumpers. She wanted to know where the second hand things had come from. Mum put me through an inquisition the Criminal Investigating Branch would have been proud of if Mum had been a Police Officer. I have never been able to tell lies: I have always believed it is far easier to tell the truth and because of this I was soon in trouble. I told her what I had done, and why I had to do it. But still she belted me. Mum was most probably thinking that she could have bought a lot of beer for four shillings and had a party with her friends.

Some time after that incident, I had three very large boils growing on my neck, which I had been suffering with for a real long time. My mother had used sulphur and dripping to treat it.

Pus was everywhere as she was really rough with me, purposely, because she knew the pain was unbearable.

In the morning, Mum sat me on the steps outside the kitchen and with a sharp needle, iodine and clean rags she proceeded to squeeze the core from the boils. If you've never had boils then you would not understand how painful they are. I tried not to scream as Mum squeezed real hard. She was determined to get the core from each boil. She'd stop now and then to place a hot cloth over the boils. As I write this, I can still remember how painful this operation was.

The next day Mum was feeling sorry for being so rough with me. She must have felt very guilty because she gave Neville and me two pennies to buy a penny ice cream each. We could have saved the pennies for a trick we often played on the grocer. With silver frost paint I'd paint the pennies all over and try to pass them off as two shilling pieces. Sadly all good things must end and end and this trick soon did. One day he looked at the silver coated penny closely and with a smile on his face he told me only criminals do this. He impressed on me that this was a bad thing to do. He was a good man and kept it secret, never telling Mum.

He knew we were having problems, as did everyone else. They all knew Mum neglected us: she had a bad reputation. They knew that when you're desperate you do very desperate things. Sometimes the grocer would see me playing on the street or throwing a tennis ball against the side wall of his shop. He would enquire where Mum was. Sometimes he and his wife asked me personal things, and I would tell him the truth. "Are you hungry?" he would ask, and I would reply: "I'm always hungry. I could eat a horse."

Calling his wife to get the crusts off the sandwich bread ends, they would put butter thinly spread and some pickles on them. The pickled crusts were beaut, and we really appreciated their kindness. I know he cared about Neville and me, because sometimes he would walk out on the street and watch us playing, then walk over and give us a lolly each, say nothing and just walk back into the shop. He was a wonderful, kind-hearted man. I'd sometimes ask him could I sweep the footpath outside his shop. We liked each other. Mum used to book up her groceries each week and he had a book with Mum's name. He would itemise all the things Mum bought and place the price in a column to the right, then when Mum came into pay, he would add up the cost. When paid, he would give Mum the list then move her to another page.

5

Church life

We were often called heathens by those who thought they were better than we were. Maybe they were. Maybe they just thought they were. If poverty makes you a heathen then most of us in Erskineville were heathens. I never believed we were heathens because I believed in Jesus, and I was taught he was ever so forgiving. God only knows I wanted to be forgiven, considering I was stealing clothes and milk from our neighbours.

Mum decided that we kids should be more involved in the Church, so she made arrangements for our baptism at Holy Trinity Church of England in Rochford Street. I was nine and Neville was six. Mum and Ma Kate were there and the Reverend Noble put the water over our heads and welcomed us as God's children. After that we went to Church every Sunday with threepence each for the plate. Sometimes we would spend a penny or two on lollies as we walked to Church, but we always made sure we kept at least a penny for Jesus. We used to love singing the hymns. In the afternoon we went to Sunday school, which was real beaut.

The Reverend Noble must have liked my singing, because he invited me to sing in the Choir. I thought they must be hard up wanting me in the Choir. But Mum gave in to the Minister's request and I enjoyed it. I felt real good with a nice white smock over my shirt. I stayed there for a while but left because I got bored. Soon we were wagging Church and spending all the plate money on lollies. Both of us were truly really bad devils spending God's money. I did feel guilty, but the taste of lollies made me forget my guilt. Sometimes we did make an appearance with no money. Sometimes we would just hang around the shops on Erskineville Road.

But I always knew when the Church picnics were on, and never missed them. I also played cricket for the Church. I was around the youngest boy in the team. For many games I would come in to bat around number nine and would usually score quick runs. I kept telling the older boys and the Minister that I should be batting further up the batting order, because I was a better batsman than most of them in front of me. They probably thought I was very egotistical, but all I wanted was to score runs and win games. I often taunted the older boys, especially Astley who was the Captain. "Why don't you put the team first and have me open and drop yourself down the order?" I would yell out when he made no runs.

After the first season of this I told them that if their thinking didn't change, they wouldn't have me. When the next cricket season came around they moved me up to number three in the batting order. We all relished the rewards, with me usually scoring fast runs and putting us in a position to win nearly all our games that year.

We loved the Sunday school picnics. We would visit places such as Parsley Bay, Balmoral Beach or go to various beaches around Cronulla. Because we loved the water these were great days. The Royal National Park was another favourite spot. There would be a picnic lunch and we would have soft drinks and sweets. We had running races and swimming races and prizes were given to the winners.

At the end of the year at the Church we would have a Special Prize Service and after the service we were given our award. They would have a party and there were sandwiches, cakes, lollies and drinks. The kids who saved the most Scripture cards received the best prizes. And then those who behaved best received special awards, which were brand new Bibles. I never won a Bible, but I had one that I bought up at the St Vinnies secondhand shop in Newtown.

One day the Reverend Noble came knocking on our front door and Mum answered it and spoke to him. I knew it was about us. Mum did not say anything about the visit. But after the Minister's visit she never got us ready for Church or gave us the money for Jesus. This lasted for only a short time: because we were in her way on Sundays while she and her boyfriends had their drunken sex orgies, she soon relented and sent us to Church again.

I will always remember one special event outside St Mary's Church when we were heading down to Woolloomooloo to do some fishing. We needed to buy some hooks but had no money, so we had this bright idea on how to make some easy money. We went inside the cathedral, which was packed out, and found some paper on a desk and some pencils. Our bright idea was starting to become a reality as my mate Dave wrote on the paper: "PLEASE HELP ME FOR I AM BLIND."

After what seemed to be a long time, all the congregation came out and began walking past us, looking at Dave with his sign in front and with his eyes closed pretending he was blind. We had a small box we found in the Cathedral and we were singing out: "Help the blind." A few Catholics stopped and asked us what were we doing. We replied we were asking for money for the blind. Poor Dave stumbled around acting the goat with his eyes shut, but he didn't fool anybody. A few good Catholics stopped and gave us a few pence, feeling sorry for us. I recall them laughing as they tried to act serious about poor blind Dave. We soon had enough money for hooks and off we went. Poor Dave was upset and wanted to know what he would say when he went to confession next time.

To get a little spending money, I would go around the streets and look for drink bottles and if I found any I would return them to the shops for the deposit. Sometimes I would go around to Armstrong's Timber Factory with my wheat bag and fill it up to the top with wood cut-offs and sell it to a few regular customers I had for one shilling a bag. Armstrong's gave me the wood for nothing.

We found another way of making money. In John Street near the old Church was Mackenzie's Rag Merchants, where a bag of rags could get us up to four shillings depending on the weight. We would go door to door asking people for any old rags they did not want. When our bag was full we would take half out and pour half a bucket of water over them and then place the other half into the bag. With some wet it weighed more. We would carry it down to the rag factory. Here they would weigh it and have us sign the book. They would give us a bag to replace our one that they kept. But it was not long before they woke up to our scheme, and after that they would always empty the rags out on the scales, giving us our own bag back plus any wet rags.

Not to be outwitted by their discovery of wet rags, we placed a nine-pound house brick in the centre of the rags, which they discovered the first time. "What's this brick doing here?" asked Mr Mackenzie. We acted dumb, and he laughed as he took it off the heap of rags. "You'll have to get up early to fool me," he said. So thereafter we became honest rag collectors and he was happy to do business with us until he closed down a few years later.

6

Escape attempt

It was around this period that Mum met Victor Fewre, who became her new boyfriend. Ma had moved out and Victor Fewre had moved in. There was a slight improvement in our living conditions at 39 Albert Street: the drinking was not as bad. Vic seemed to be all right, but the improvement soon faded away and Mum and Vic and their drinking and fighting had us concerned. I know Vic was deeply fond of Mum: he bought her a Beale pianola and gave her anything that she wanted.

The two of them would sit in the front room playing the pianola and singing songs from the rolls where all the words were displayed. I recall some of their favourite songs: *Harbour Lights*, *I Believe*, *When You're In Love*, and *Roses of Picardy*. They also had some new 78 records. Even though the drinking and arguments returned, one consolation was that they were not as violent.

But then one night Vic and Mum had a real big fight. Mum had been drinking big time. Suddenly Vic reached for his hat and coat and walked out, saying he was never returning, and off he went. After a few minutes, Mum realised what she had done and how stupid she had been. She sent us after Vic, telling us to beg him to come back. We caught up to Vic as he reached Erskineville Road just near the Hub number two theatre.

We begged Vic to come back with us. He could see we were sincere in wanting him back: we knew how much better things had been since he had moved in. But reluctantly he said: "No." It was about 11 going on 12 o'clock and here we were grabbing his hands, trying to persuade him to return with us. But he was not going to change his mind. We watched him get on the bus home to his mother's place at Piper Street, Lilyfield.

Neville and I walked home in fear, knowing we would be terrorised by Mum. We were not to be disappointed. Mum gave us hell. She abused us and bashed us and with her usual foul language had us stand in the centre of the room, taunting us with her gutter talk. She then made us stand in the corner until near daylight.

Neville and I had had enough. We made plans to run away and we immediately began to put our plan into action. We secured an old English-style cane pram behind my pushbike, held by a pole and rope tied to the bike's seat. We put a pot and a pan and a few plates and a little bread and some cereals and whatever other food we could find into the pram. We took the two army blankets and then we set off, not really knowing where we were going. One of us would walk while the other rode the bike and when the hills became too steep we both pushed the bike and pram.

By about six o'clock we reached Bankstown and were worn out. We realised having the pram was too much to push, so we discarded the old pram near Bankstown Railway Station.

Later that night we rode off the road into an open area underneath trees and fell asleep in long tall grass so as not to be seen from the road. In the morning we awoke to the singing of wild birds in the trees around us. Some of these birds were new to us: they were all colours and their whistles echoed all around us. It was beautiful. We washed in a watercourse and sat down and ate dry bread and some dry cereals.

We were lost and soon got tired of walking in the hot sun, and with only a few biscuits left we were hungry. I was worried and frightened but Neville was not: he was adamant he did not want to return home. We rode double on the bike on the flat and downhill and kept going on the main road. That afternoon we reached the outskirts of Picton.

It was getting dark and we had no food left, and no money either. We built a cover from the branches around us near a creek, which we drank water from. We soon fell asleep and next thing we realised it was morning.

Later that day we got a large hole in the front tyre and the chain kept breaking beyond repair, so we dumped the bike beside the road. We waved a truck down and asked the driver had he seen any road gangs: Neville said some road gang men had once told him life on the road was great, and if we ever saw them we would be welcome to set up camp with them. But the driver said no, he hadn't seen any. He offered us a lift, and later when we saw a road gang the driver let us out.

We spoke to a few men, but they had no idea who Neville was talking about. We were very upset and hungry, which the men noticed. They offered us a few sandwiches, which we ate very quickly and then left them, off down the highway with our blankets over our shoulder. We must have looked a sight.

It was inevitable we had to return home, so we tried to get a lift, with many trucks just driving past us. Then a large truck stopped. The driver asked us what we were doing alone on such a hot day. We told him everything. He invited us to drive with him as he was going to Sydney.

After a few miles he stopped at a shop and came back with a

few sandwiches and a drink each of beautiful ginger beer. He was a real good bloke and was a good talker, telling us funny things he often saw on the road. He laughed about our bike and pram and how we had to discard it piece by piece. He asked us were we a belated part of the Blaxland, Lawson and Wentworth party that crossed the Blue Mountains in 1813. We laughed and so did he when I said we were not born then.

Next thing he said: "Well boys, this is where I have to drop you off, at St Peters Railway Station." We assured him it was not far from home. His last words were: "Go straight home boys: I'm sure your mother is worried sick." Previously, he had spoken about dropping us at Newtown Police Station because of his great concern of what could happen to us. We promised him we were going straight home because we were very hungry and worn out.

Well we arrived home and found the front door key and let ourselves in. It was easy to get in as Mum always had the key hidden under a pot plant on the verandah and if the key was not there, all we had to do was climb up on the laundry roof then pull ourselves to the second level and open the unlocked window to our bedroom: the lock on the window had broken years ago and this gave us the freedom to come and go unnoticed. We had done this hundreds of times.

First thing we did was search the food cupboard for anything that resembled food. We found some bread, so we put the frying pan on, melted the dripping and made fried bread and sprinkled salt and a little tomato sauce on it. We stayed in the house and did not go out, not wanting to be seen. We were worried what Mum and Vic – who had relented and returned to live with Mum while we were on the run – would have to say. Had they contacted the police and reported us missing? Hesitant and scared, we did not want Mum to know we had come home, so we cleaned up our mess very diligently.

We then went and hid behind the Beale pianola, which was situated on an angle in the corner of the front room. We must have dozed off, for next thing we heard voices and recognised Mum and Vic and Flossie Forest, one of Mum's best friends who lived about six doors up in the next block.

In hindsight we could not have found a worse place to hide, because they were soon all gathered around the pianola singing and drinking. This went on for hours, then Flossie went home and Mum and Vic seemed like they were getting ready for bed. Everything went quiet and soon they both came into the front room, yelling at us to come out from behind the pianola.

How on earth did they know we were there? I thought we were well hidden and very quiet. So very gingerly we came out, and the looks on their faces were strange. We must have looked like scraggy, dirty looking kids like Charles Dickens' Oliver Twist. We sure felt like that and with Mother being that horrible Fagan. And boy did she lay into us and give us one hell of a beating. With us black and blue she told us to get to bed. She was not concerned that we were hungry and in need of a warm bath. Later we found out they had found our blankets on the lounge: we had forgotten to hide them. During their drinking they had noticed us behind the pianola without us having any idea or realising we had been seen.

SCHOOL LIFE

It was a new school year at Erskineville Primary. After assembly everyone was placed in new classes with a few new teachers. I was put in a new class called "Opportunity Class" for kids that were behind in their learning. The teacher, Mr Laws, was a tall skinny man, always very upright. I believe he was an old Army man. He had thinning red hair and a lot of sunspots over his face.

From the moment I went into his class I instinctively knew

I would like it. There was no ego with Mr Laws. He had an egalitarian system in place and he would explain things clearly, making sure everyone understood.

I recall our very first lesson was on the emancipation of our convict ancestors and how downtrodden they were and how in desperate poverty they were forced to steal to feed their families in England, Scotland and Ireland. To give all of us a better understanding, Mr Laws would have us dramatise it by acting out various parts, showing how we thought the convicts would have felt.

All of us took turns at being class boy, with the usual duties of filling inkwells and cleaning the blackboard. As a reward, the class boy would receive a bag with a piece of cake and some fruit. At the end of the month he would choose the best class boy, and the winner would receive a book as a prize.

Mr Laws imbued into all of us the need to do our best, and he gave us the incentive to do better. I have never tried so much in all of my life, and was rewarded a few times as "class boy of the month". To me it was a great honour. We all could see Mr Laws was very proud of his class. We respected him so much: we would do anything for him, for we knew he was a very concerned teacher doing his best for us.

Mr Laws was a fantastic teacher with innovative ideas but always starting from the basics. His methods were slow and methodical. As we picked up, the faster learners would assist the slower boys. Say, for instance, a boy was unsure about something. He would be brought to the blackboard to observe as the other boys would come out to complete the answer, explaining what they were doing to reach it. With this method you were forced to observe with complete concentration at all times, because you could be the next boy called out.

Mr Laws encouraged creativity, and if he asked a question he wanted everyone's hands up. If he noticed a boy who had not put

Come home, you little bastards

his hand up, that boy would have it explained by the boys who knew, then the boy would front the class and give the answer. The method was for total concentration.

History was Mr Laws' favourite subject. He often said: "History teaches us who we really are." He would teach us to read everything concerning our history and then he would tell the class more about what we had read.

Then would come our favourite part: dramatising the story. During the acting Mr Laws would choose who he thought portrayed the part best. That chosen boy was given an early mark. Often boys declined the early mark, because they were having so much fun acting in the play. He certainly made us enthusiastic and dedicated to learning. Often we would just stay back talking to him about anything that was happening in our lives.

Very seldom did he have to use the cane, but the few boys who misbehaved and were caned always acknowledged they deserved it and there was never any animosity. We were never caned unless it was a serious breach of the rules. The punishment was accepted and everyone was still a great mate, because we all regarded Mr Laws as a mate.

Sometimes if a boy was having learning difficulties, Mr Laws would arrange for that boy to have lunch in the classroom or after school. This was voluntary on the boy's part, but with no exceptions they would take up this special offer. I learned so much by this special offer from such a dedicated teacher. Yes, I eulogise about Mr Laws, simply because without his special teaching methods and dedication I don't know how I would have turned out.

When the first half yearly test results came in, I was so delighted I ran home to tell Mum of my good marks. Mum did not even bother to look, which truly disappointed me. She could not care less.

After the good reports from the half yearly exams, I was determined to do even better. I tried very hard and participated in everything. As the year moved on I was really improving and so was my arithmetic. This was because Mr Laws was giving me extra tuition during lunch breaks.

I did once receive the cane from Mr Laws. One morning whilst playing marbles, this goose of a kid ran off with some of my marbles, so I ran after him and caught him. I demanded my marbles back, but he threw them on the street. I was so angry I punched him until the goose crouched on the ground crying. Mr Laws was on playground duty. He dragged me off the kid. He asked no questions, and told us both to wait outside our classroom. While waiting, I warned the goose: "Don't you ever come near me again or next time I'll rip your head off." The goose never uttered a single word.

Soon all the class was seated and Mr Laws called us in, saying: "Do you want to go to the headmaster or accept a sixer from me?" We both decided on the sixer from him. The goose went first and after three heavy laid cuts, he started to bawl. I took my sixer without any fuss, even though my hands were in terrible pain. I could not hold my pen to write, and I just sulked at my desk for most of the day.

Mr Laws had a way of making people relaxed and very soon he had me laughing at a joke about marbles relating to the goose and me. Later that day he called me out front to show the class my history book and heaped praise on me for a supreme effort. He would place a hand on your shoulder and pat your back. The goose brought his father to school next day and the boys heard Mr Laws say: "Your son started the fight by stealing the boy's marbles, who then chased him, only for your son to throw them across the street, so he deserved what he got."

The yearly test examination of all our subjects began. I was confident of doing well and I did. A week before the Christmas break, Mr Laws called me out front, approached me and placed his hand on my shoulder, telling the class I had come first. He said that I had shown a dedication by putting in extra time at school and at home. He said: "I had been told by other teachers Carl Beauchamp had been a difficult boy to teach because he lacked concentration and had a myriad of home problems caused by his mother's lifestyle." Mr Laws went on to say how proud he was of me for showing dedication to my studies under such difficult conditions at home and for proving his innovative teaching methods worked. I recall how happy I was listening to what Mr Laws said about me; he had a way of doing this that made you feel good about yourself. I have never forgotten his kindness.

The Christmas holidays came and went. I was now 12 years old and moving into high school. I was sent to Newtown Technical School. Life can be so sad: just as you become happy for the first time at school you have to move on to further life experiences. I hated Newtown from the very first day. A Mr Wiltshire was the headmaster. This bastard was in love with himself. Mr Narcissism was what the boys called him, among other malicious names such as Poofter. You avoided him like the plague. He would walk into your class unannounced and without any beg pardons just take right over without apologising to the teacher.

Life here was so different. Most of the teachers expected you to know everything and unlike Mr Laws never took time to give individual attention. I also couldn't stand the older brown-nose prefects who would calumniate the first year students like me. These prefects were the biggest mob of crawlers I had ever met in my life. I was defiant in not taking orders from them. They soon tried to take their revenge against me.

They would often come up asking to see my lunch pass, which allowed you to leave the school grounds for lunch. So if there was no good reason for them to sight it, I'd tell them to piss off, and then they would report me to Wiltshire, who in turn would want to see me in his office.

I'd explain I had already shown my pass on return and I was not going to be intimidated by his brown-nosed prefect crawlers. He disliked me and I told him I detested him. This took him by surprise and I urged him to take the matter further.

After a while I hated getting up to go to this school of crawlers, so I started to wag school and before long I was missing two and three days a week, only turning up on the good days when we had sport. I used to write my own notes for days missed, signing my mother's name. I used every possible excuse, like mother being ill or deaths in the family or that someone was near death in hospital.

7

Before the Children's Court

One day I was called to Headmaster Wiltshire's office and spoken to about my absenteeism. Out of nowhere he produced my notes. He gave me a letter to give to my mother. I read it on the way home, and seeing it was not complimentary I tore it up and threw it away.

Later I was called to the headmaster's office again and this time with the headmaster was a Truant Inspector. He spoke of all my missed school days and produced all my handwritten notes, which he implied I had written myself and asked why my mother had not contacted the school. "Did you give your mother the letter and did she receive by mail any letters?" he asked. Well I knew about them all because I had ripped all of them up. I was keeping one step ahead and keeping Mum in the dark. I just ignored their questions, which had them so confused they were stuttering and unable to find words to express themselves.

Nothing changed and I only attended school when I felt like it, mostly staying home and sometimes going to Circular Quay or Woolloomooloo Wharf where with my fishing line I'd try to catch some fish. Sometimes if I had any money I'd go to see a movie or just walk around the City.

Later that year the Child Welfare caught up with Mum and she had to bring me with her to the Newtown office, which was opposite the Post Office near King Street. It was a second-floor, dirty, shabby office. The inspectors spoke with Mum about my wagging school and produced all my notes. They asked me questions, which I refused to answer. There was not much I could say: the game was up.

They also produced a few letters from people who lived near us. They had reported very unfavourable events and accused us of being uncontrollable and stated our mother was never home. They said our house was a "den of iniquity" and a "brothel". They accused Neville and me of stealing their milk money and clothing from their washing lines. They said we often had girls living with us at the house whilst Mum was away days and weeks at a time. This was only partly true: we did have girls dropping into our house, but they did not stay over. Because of my mother's exploits I was an early learner when it came to sex, but at this stage I was still on my L-plates or maybe my P-plates.

The Child Welfare officials also said we played loud music all the time on our record player; and that often we were drunk on our mother's home-made beer. Our mother agreed with them, except for any charges that were unfavourable to her. Mum did not stand up for us in any possible way.

The police had also made contact with Mum, telling her we often brought our girlfriends into the house when she was at work and that one of the girls, Joan, was pregnant. I was real fond of Joan and she often came to see me alone and with one episode leading to another, things did happen. I often told Joan she was my favourite girlfriend and after that she was always coming in to see me. So when Joan fell pregnant I took the blame, even though I had no way of knowing for sure if it was my baby: they claimed my mates had also had sex with Joan quite often and also boys from George Street, Erskineville, but I did not know at the time if that was correct.

Me and my two best mates had to go to Ashfield Police Station to talk to the police about our sexual adventures. Joanie was placed in a Home in Ashfield to have her baby. I never saw her again.

A little later all of us received letters to appear at the Yasmar Children's Court at Ashfield over our sexual misbehaviour and missing school and being uncontrollable. They forgot to mention being badly neglected.

From this moment on, both my life and Neville's were to change.

My friends were also in court. When the Magistrate asked if the parents would take closer care of them if they were released, all the other parents said yes. They and their parents listened as Mum said Neville and I were uncontrollable and she could not manage us, and made herself out to be an angel. But they all knew Mum was just a liar. The parent of one of the girls spoke out and said: "As far as Carl being uncontrollable, maybe the Court would be better served by taking a closer look at his Mum."

What a hypocrite Mum was: she did not give Neville or me any support.

The outcome was the others were all placed on bonds to be of good behaviour for three years.

The consequence for Neville and me was that we were charged with being "uncontrollable" by Child Welfare. I was taken to the Yasmar Correctional Centre or "Shelter" as it was called at Ashfield. This was a place where children waited until they appeared in the Yasmar Children's Court. I don't know where they sent Neville: I did not see him again until we both went to court.

The Yasmar Shelter was established at Haberfield by the Department of Community Services as a remand home for boys. Yasmar was located in a fine old private house, which the NSW government bought in 1944 and it became a centre for juvenile justice. Timber structures were erected on the former tennis court and croquet lawns to house delinquent boys. The grand reception rooms of the house became a children's court and others served as magistrates' rooms. The name Yasmar came about because the property where Yasmar stands was once the property of a Mr Ramsay, a well-to-do person in his time. If you spell Ramsay backwards, you have "Yasmar."

Yasmar was full of young kids from broken and dysfunctional families. Often the children were not accompanied to Yasmar Court by their parents, only the Child Welfare Officer. This person usually blamed the children, who had no voice in Court and were mostly charged with being "uncontrollable". The court never gave children the opportunity to tell how life really was.

Poor wretched children were confronted by high and mighty magistrates who nearly always blamed them. These types of judiciary people were endemic during these years, when "a child was to be seen and not heard". These old ways should have been corrected a hundred years ago, but instead it's just plodded on with children made to take the full blame for the mistakes of their parents and their parents before them.

As I type these words, tears are flowing down onto my keyboard. I feel the pain as my chest tightens: the emotional side of it just will not go away.

A boy's love for his mother is unconditional. She could be deceitful, ungenerous, mean, depraved, iniquitous, unloving. It did not matter: she was still my mother.

At Yasmar, I was sexually molested by an officer. He watched me in the shower and as I attempted to dry myself he started to fondle me and then he led my hand to his erect penis and forced me to masturbate him. Later after he was sexually gratified he took me back to my bed where, with nobody else around, he tried to rape me. He ordered me to undress and lie face first on the bed. I made it very difficult for him, so he could not fully penetrate me. He hurt me, and I was very frightened: Yasmar was a very tough, regimented environment, where we were discouraged from saying anything unless spoken to first. I said nothing, and just tried to always avoid the officer who had raped me.

This officer, George Hatton, later went to work at Carlingford Boys' Home. Neville was in the Carlingford Home during those years, staying until he was about 14 years old. Neville later returned home but he could not stand Mum so he moved out and boarded with a Mrs Hatton, George's mother, in Redfern. I found out 55 years later that George was doing the same thing to boys at Carlingford Boys' Home.

Why didn't I cry out to draw attention to the assault? This question has often been put to me. To put it simply, I was intimidated by his power over me in such an unfriendly environment.

After being in the Yasmar Correctional Centre for four or five weeks, our court case finally came up. I watched Mum in Court: she could not hide from me what she was thinking and not saying, as she spoke to the Children's Magistrate. She tried to make out that she was such a good mother. I could see she was taking this opportunity to get rid of us.

The Children's Court Magistrate was an old man named Mr Frank Murphy. I recall him saying, "Well, it is obvious to me Mrs Beauchamp that you want to unload your children on to someone else!" He then said: "I have no doubt they are both uncontrollable, but they are also badly neglected and are in danger." You could see he was not impressed with Mum's attitude. He even said that if we had been given a little love and attention and if she had been home more to look after us, he had no doubt none of us would be there that day.

Then he said: "For your own good, Carl and Neville, I will be sending you to separate Church Homes. This has been kindly arranged by the Court Chaplain, Reverend Ray Weir. Neville, you will be going to Carlingford and Carl will be going to Charlton Boy's Home at Glebe, both controlled by the Church of England."

I did not like being separated from Neville and I told the Magistrate. I also said that if our mother had cared about us more then maybe we would not have gotten ourselves into this trouble.

I was in great pain this day, because I just did not know how I could tell Magistrate Murphy of what George Hatton had done to me. How could I explain how Mr Hatton molested me? I wanted to speak out, but my lips would not open. I also thought he would probably not believe me anyway: how could I expect him to take the word of an uncontrollable child? But why didn't he ask me how I was getting on in the Detention Centre? If he did ask me, maybe I would have spoken out and in hindsight this may have prevented further attacks at Charlton.

The Magistrate then said that to prevent us being locked up any further at Yasmar, the court chaplain, Reverend Ray Weir, would drive me to Charlton and Neville to Carlingford straight away. He asked Mum to arrange for our personal belongings and clothing to be brought to the Homes. This had to be a joke as we had very little of anything. He said Neville was to go away until he was 14 and I until I was 16. I was 13 years old at this time and Neville was 10.

8

Life in Charlton

On arrival at Charlton Boys' Home in Glebe, the chaplain, Reverend Weir, took Mum and me into the office of the superintendent, Mr Norman Sachisthal, who greeted us with a take-it-or-leave-it "Hello". The first things I noticed were his grey spikey crewcut hair and his belly protruding a little. He then began to give us information on how the Home operated and the rules. He said on a number of occasions that he was not to be messed with.

Sachisthal then asked Mum about the child endowment she received and told Mum it was to be paid to the Home. We then walked outside and around to the side entrance door where the Chaplain's car was, and waved goodbye as the Chaplain and Mum drove off, heading to Yasmar again to pick Neville up for the trip to Carlingford.

Sachisthal then gave me a tour of the Home, pointing out different rules and such. We went into the kitchen where I met Miss Craig the cook and Mrs Campbell and Matron Sachisthal, the superintendent's wife. Then Sachisthal introduced me to Mr

Norman, who was a short, nuggetty Englishman who had a broad English accent: his pronunciation of words was hard to understand. He was very fit, and I could see immediately he had a good sense of humour.

Sachisthal then gave me pyjamas, new clothing, shoes and a new grey suit, which he emphasised must be looked after as this was "Sunday Best" for Church on Sundays. I was thrilled to be given so much so soon. He said I would be expected to do chores, and that I would go to Glebe Technical School. He said the gate was never locked but should I ever choose to abscond, he would not accept me back. He emphasised Mount Penang Correctional Centre would be my next port of call if I misbehaved, adding: "This port of call you don't want." Sachisthal said: "Carl, do everything the best you can, that is all I ask of you. Don't you dare give me reason to give you a hiding."

I soon began to fit in to my new Charlton life. Good meals, a nice warm bed and nice clean clothing and shoes for ordinary wear and a pair for church and special occasions.

Soon after arriving and being judged a well-behaved and trusted boy, Sachisthal called me to his office. Here, he told me he was pleased with me and asked me about my previous life at home with Mum. I told him what my home life was like, and soon I was in an uncontrollable emotional state. He came out from behind his desk and placed his hand on my head, showing what seemed like real sympathy as he led me out of the office.

Chores in Charlton were rostered. Everyone took turns at washing and wiping up after each meal and cleaning the pots and pans. This was separate from your normal chores of dormitory cleaning, polishing with wax the floors throughout the building, daily laundry work such as washing and drying and folding, general sweeping of the yards etc. There was no doubt Sachisthal and his staff were brilliant organisers.

The buildings were always spotless because no one was

allowed to be idle. Even if the floors were shining bright, he'd give you rags to improve the shine. These chores were for everyone before and after school. Working boys did not have to do as many chores but had to keep their rooms tidy and clean. These rooms were in the Strathmore Building, which was being refurbished. The working boys sometimes supervised the work of the schoolboys.

On a Monday everyone was up at 6am. Everyone would put their working clothes on, make their beds and clean and tidy the dormitories. When this was completed we would go to the showers and toilet blocks; here we often had a cold shower, as the kitchen had priority on all hot water. When the washing and showering were finished, everyone would go to their daily chores – kitchen, dining room or floor polishing – while others would be getting breakfast ready under the supervision of the cooking staff. Some boys would be setting out the plates, cups and cutlery.

Other boys would be cleaning up the shower and toilet blocks and hand basins and cleaning the floor. Others would go with Mr Norman on project jobs, such as building the planned basketball area from scratch. This was hard work, rolling heavy sandstone blocks from the furthest corner of the Home, all uphill. These sandstone blocks would be precisely placed to form a retaining wall, which was around 15 feet high at the lowest level.

Some of these blocks were well over a ton and would take up to a dozen boys working in relay to roll them end-on-end up and then position them correctly in the wall. Some blocks were six feet long by over 18 inches across. Mr Norman had devised various systems to move them, and an ingenious pulley and plank system for levering them up on top of each other. But it was hard, backbreaking work. We used crowbars and brute force. One consolation: it made us fit. All of our hands were cut, bruised and blistered by this convict style work: it was so painful it was hard to even hold a shovel or any other tool for that matter. At school we sometimes found it profoundly difficult to write, which the teachers quickly noticed.

One teacher who noticed how badly bruised my hands were was Mr Jack Moroney. He laughed as he said: "Well, you won't be caned on the hand with such injured hands but your arse will feel the pain if you do the wrong thing."

He was my maths teacher and by coincidence had also been my maths teacher at Newtown Tech: he joined my new school, Glebe Tech, at about the time I started there. Moroney was a very good cricketer and represented Australia. He told me not to worry if my writing was bad, as he was taking into account how profoundly bruised my hands were. He personally contacted Sachisthal and explained the situation and offered advice, saying he should pay more attention so that the Home boys were not injured doing hard labour.

We were given an incentive by Sachisthal: we were allowed to go to the Astor Theatre on Glebe Point Road once a month if we all worked diligently doing our wall building. This basketball project took us over 12 months of backbreaking work, and it was a great joy when it was finished.

At 7.30am the bells would ring and we would rush to the shower block to wash our dirty hands. We would then proceed to the assembly hall and line up. Then under Sachisthal's orders and a daily lecture we would proceed to the dining room in an orderly, no-talking fashion for breakfast. We would move to our respective tables and stand directly behind our usual chair until told to be seated by Sachisthal. The staff table was near the exit to the kitchen. It had six chairs and a tablecloth. The inmates' tables were plain, maple coloured timbers. We never had tablecloths.

Sachisthal would then issue instructions for each day before he sat down to join the other staff members. Then he would chastise those who he believed were in need of a lecture, which could go on for 10 minutes or so. He would then have us say 'grace' in parrot-like fashion: "For what we are about to receive, may the Lord make us truly grateful." I have always thought that saying grace should come from the heart with your own words, rather than being recited in an ordered fashion.

Breakfast consisted of a cereal and two slices of bread with golden syrup but no butter, and then a foul-tasting cup of tea. I always thought it had a thing called bromide added to prevent the boys being randy, as young men have high testosterone levels. I noticed the same taste when some years later I was called up for National Service in the Army at Ingleburn: very fit young men being given bromide mixed furtively with their drinks.

In winter we had porridge every day. Milk, when we had it, came in large blue jugs for use on cereals such as Weet Bix. The plates and cups during my time over three years never changed: all plastic and greyish yellow in colour.

After everyone had finished eating, Sachisthal would dismiss all the boys to continue their chores. Then at 8.15am everyone would wash up, clean their teeth and get ready for school, then proceed with their school bag to pick up their brown paper bag with marmite or jam sandwiches for lunch.

Then you walked to school, choosing to walk with whoever you liked. The rules forbade you from calling into shops. In any case we didn't have any money. You were not allowed to dawdle and had to go straight to school: some of us to Glebe Technical High School and others to Forest Lodge or Glebe Primary School. I was in first year to start with and I found all the boys friendlier than at Newtown Technical High School.

After school, we all had to go straight back to the Home. If you were not through the gates by a certain time, Sachisthal would punish you. At times he was brutal, more so with some than others. You could lose your enjoyment activity as well. His most common punishment was no sweets for a week.

On return to the home, you would go to your dormitory and change into working clothes and swiftly proceed to your afternoon chores. But before going to chores, you would go to outside the kitchen and help yourself to a cup of bromide tea and a cake or a scone or a sandwich. You then worked until 5pm, got cleaned up and assembled in the main hall. You would be called to fall in, then march to the dining room. Here you always stood at the back of your chair. Sachisthal would speak of one thing or another, and then tell you to be seated. Grace was said and then you would eat your meal, usually two courses.

The meals were nothing fancy but were nourishing. In winter there would always be soups and there were sweets of tapioca or sago or custard, a piece of bread with syrup and a piece of fruit and a cup of tea. The bread was often grain bread and sometimes we had a little margarine. Miss Craig most nights had celery soup on our limited menu. She was a person who could make meals out of anything. If she had heaps of onions then we had onion soup every day until the onions had been used up, or the celery used up.

After dinner, which was then called "tea", we filled in time doing whatever we liked if we did not have kitchen duty. At around 7pm we would assemble in the main hall, then proceed to do gymnastics in the last building on the property, which was furthest west. Here Mr Keating from the YMCA would take gymnastics classes. This continued until about 9pm. One of his friends, Bob Davies, also took gymnastics. Even from the beginning I knew this bloke was a paedophile, as his hands would feel your private parts and backside as he assisted you in various exercises. What a slime he was!

We had a gymnastics horse, which we vaulted over doing handstands and double twists, jumping from a springboard. Every boy was expected to perform and God help those who did not try their best: Sachisthal would watch and be ruthless in enforcing uniformity. After Keating or Davies dismissed us, we would clean up and retire to our beds. Sometimes Davies would keep one boy back for "extra fine-tuning", which we all knew was to touch the boy up and to do other sexual things without being seen by anyone.

For some time after my arrival at Charlton, on a Tuesday night two elderly couples who lived in Glebe came to teach all the boys "Old Time Dancing" and another elderly man would play the piano. Each boy had to have a partner and so we had boys dancing together, each taking turns of taking the boy's part. All the boys had to do the dancing classes. The two elderly couples would do each dance while we watched, and later we would be invited onto the floor to dance the Pride of Erin, the gypsy tap and the barn dance.

During the dance the teachers would take each boy in turn and show us the finer points of the dance. They were relentless in pointing out our mistakes. I must admit these teachers were very good and all of us boys loved watching how light they were on their feet: they were so smooth with their turns. They made us look so amateur: as they danced they were so graceful compared to us, all feet and falling over ourselves.

As the weeks went by, all of us boys became much better at doing the basic steps. None of us could do the professional-looking steps of our teachers. So on the weekly Saturday dance night all of us boys were quick to show the girls how well we danced. All the girls from the Young People's Club, which was a club Sachisthal had formed for encouraging outside boys and girls in the neighbourhood to get involved in some social activities at Charlton, would comment to us on how good we were at dancing.

One Saturday night, Sachisthal made a speech on the dancing progress we had made, and he thanked our elderly teachers. The teachers came on stage and they complimented us on being good students. Without warning or Sachisthal's approval, they then invited the outside boys and girls to join us at the Tuesday night dance lessons. This became a regular thing for a few more months and gave all of us heaps of happiness. On our last lesson, Sachisthal thanked our teachers and gave each of them a gift, saying it was from the boys and girls of the Young People's Club.

After tea on Wednesdays we had the Wednesday Young People's Club Games Night, or occasionally an Old Time Dance Night. My mother visited a few times but not very often. The local teenage boys and girls and the girls from nearby Bidura Girls' Home would join us in the dancing. It was great to dance with the girls, who made all of us feel good to be able to talk and have our secretive chats of telling the girls how we liked them and steal a kiss here and there.

We were able to mix openly with the girls, as long as we observed the rules. These rules were obvious and a careful watch saw no boys and girls leave the hall together. I believe this was why they mixed bromide in our tea. I never dared break the rules. We were all placed on trust, and to break this trust would see everyone punished. You could be ostracised by your fellow inmates and you could see the leather whip brought out by Sachisthal. Two of my friends broke the rules and they told me how they kissed and did other things quickly with the girls. How they did this was by pretending they were sick and getting permission to go to bed. But instead of that they would wait outside in the dark for their girlfriends to come outside, pretending to go to the toilet.

Thursday nights everyone assembled in the hall. Here Sachisthal would take a religious service. We had our own Charlton Young Peoples' Club Chaplain who wore his or her white large ribbon around the neck. The Chaplain would assist Sachisthal by reading a few selected verses from the Holy Bible. We would sing the selected hymns and Sachisthal would give a sermon: sometimes very interesting; sometimes long-winded and dull, boring everyone stupid.

Fridays were free nights. Some boys were allowed to go to the Astor Theatre on Glebe Road. These were mostly working boys or schoolboys who had got special merit awards. Everyone had to be back in the Home by 11pm. If one person broke the rules, everyone was punished.

Saturday was a 7am sleep-in. Everyone did the same chores as on weekdays. But after breakfast everyone had to line up outside the kitchen door for the weekly dose of Epsom salts, which had us running to the toilets all day. Everyone had the runs but still had to do their chores. There was always a toilet queue, with the boys in line yelling out for those in the occupied toilets to hurry up. The Epsom salts mixed with hot water were very strong; we drank quickly, so as not to taste the nasty drink.

Saturday was also the day when Mr Norman's work group achieved the most work on the construction of the basketball court area. Mr Norman would use every spare boy and no boy ever bludged, probably because Len Norman made sure nobody was idle. He was a very hard taskmaster but he led by example: he never asked anyone to do work that he would not do himself. When the retaining wall was completed, the staff had every boy take part in the Charlton Home's biggest clean-up. Later dirt filling was brought in by heavy vehicles. A heavy roller flattened the whole area and then levelled it out. It was then covered with reddish dolomite which was spread by hand by the wall gang.

When the job was completed, there was a ceremony attended by many dignitaries from the Home Mission Society, Church of England Ministers from St Andrew's in Sydney, St John's at Glebe and St Barnabas's on Broadway, Children's Court Magistrates, political officials and the Reverend Ray Weir. The Church dedicated the project and then declared it open and ready for activities. Lucky for all it was a nice sunny day, which made Sachisthal happy.

On Saturday nights we had a variety of different social activities. Sometimes Sachisthal would show some old movies. Some of these definitely came out of Noah's ark. Sometimes there would be a concert night; here outsiders would perform side by side with the inmates. Sometimes the hall would be set up for a games night. Some boys would play table tennis or use Sachisthal's billiard table in the foyer. Others would listen to the wireless or just read or catch up on schoolwork. Others on punishment would work polishing and waxing the kitchen and dining room floors.

Sundays were a day of little work but they began the same as every other day. After all basic chores were completed, everyone would get dressed for the 10am church service, mostly at St John's Bishopthorpe Church on Glebe Point Road opposite the old Glebe Post Office building. On special occasions we attended St Barnabas Church on Broadway for events such as confirmation. For a while, one of the congregation members was Arthur Stace, the man who in chalk wrote the word "Eternity" all over Sydney and the inner suburbs.

The ministers at St John's were the Reverend JP Dryland and the Reverend JFG Olds. At St Barnabas's, the ministers were the Reverend Robinson and the Reverend Howard McGuiness. The 10am service at St John's would often be a long service: it would be nearly midday when we left the Church to return to the home. Reverend Olds was a very serious old type of preacher, who at times had us falling asleep; if caught dozing off we were reported to Sachisthal for punishment. The ministers at St Barnabas's were more modern and easier to listen to.

I always found that if a minister wanted the congregation to hold on to each word spoken, the sermon had to have some relevance to what was happening in your own life. Sadly

Come home, you little bastards

Reverend Olds could not think on the level of young people. One either possesses this ability or does not.

Sometimes on the way home if we had any money or had just pretended to put our sixpence on the church collection plate, we would purposely lag well behind, making sure everyone was in front of us. We had to make sure nobody saw us as we sneaked into a shop to buy a bottle of Coke and then consume it quickly so we could catch up with the boys in front. If you were caught, you could bet Sachisthal would demonstrate his anger through his thick cane. Worse still was certain loss of leisure activities: to miss the weekly dancing and meeting outside girls was a huge price to pay.

I recall one of my friends, Barry, was dobbed in one Sunday. As he walked in the home entrance, Sachisthal was waiting for him. He was given a belting around the face and head, then dragged by the ears into the office. We could hear Sachisthal screaming out like a maniac: "You're a thief, you stole the plate money from the church, you spent the money buying sweets in the shop, you thief." Next thing my mate was screaming out in pain as Sachisthal punched him in the face. He was then dragged out into the yard by his ears and told there will be no meals for him until tomorrow. Needless to say Barry was sorry for his indiscretion and later apologised to Sachisthal. After that episode the offering plate at St John's received sixpences from every boy each week and Barry never again pretended to put it in. In fact he made an exaggerated point, so as to be noticed, of dropping the sixpence from his hand into the plate.

After a while many of us thought Sachisthal had our sixpences marked, and you would often see the boys examining the coin for markings. We were becoming a little obsessive, some suggesting that the minister counted all the sixpences and reported the tally back to Sachisthal. But it was only a matter of time before someone once again found the nerve to steal money meant for the church offering.

Keeping the hot water system going was one of the most important chores at Charlton and the boy given this chore had to be very reliable. The boy would have to be up two hours earlier than everyone else to fuel the boiler. Because it would be grossly unfair to keep the same boy looking after the boiler week in and week out, Sachisthal would appoint different boys who would be boiler boy for a few weeks only. Sachisthal often gave the boy who did this chore special privileges. I have no idea what they were because I was never boiler boy.

The kitchen staff would be up very early each day to prepare breakfast. Lunches also had to be prepared for the working boys and all those attending outside schools. So some boys who were on kitchen duty would also be up well before anyone else. They would set the table in the dining room, cooking porridge in winter or placing cereals in each bowl. A jug of milk would be placed on each table along with a bowl of sugar and golden syrup or treacle. Each boy would receive one slice of bread and of course the cups for the bromide-flavoured tea. Each boy would have his spoon for his porridge and a knife to put the syrup on his already buttered bread.

Sometimes when the kitchen staff arrived the water would not be hot and there would be havoc to pay as Mrs Craig went crook on everyone. She would then seek out the boiler boy and go crook on him. Of course Sachisthal would hear of the no hot water problem and would investigate to check whether the boy had slept in. In the opinion of the cook there was no excuse for the water not being hot.

When all the boys lined up for morning showers, if the water was cold you could hear the anguish as the boys turned the water on, especially in winter. Often the boys would also find out who the boiler boy was and when he was identified, all the boys would give it to him verbally with many threats. I never saw any justification in having a go at anyone, after all we all made mistakes and we all often wanted to sleep in for an extra 10 minutes, especially on those cold, wet winter mornings.

If the boiler boy failed in his duty he would never hear the end of it, because Sachisthal was relentless in reminding everyone that the boiler boy had failed dismally in his very important duties. Even weeks after, Sachisthal would still be reminding all of us of the boiler boy who thought it better to sleep in rather than do his duty correctly. I recall one boiler boy who neglected his duty was never allowed to have hot showers during his incarceration.

After all meals were served, there were always heaps of aluminium saucepans, frying pans, baking dishes and other utensils used in cooking meals to be washed up. Most of these were very greasy, so it was agreed in the name of hygiene that hot water was very essential for the washing of everything after meals.

For reasons unknown, there were a few boys who Sachisthal looked after as if they were his own sons. These boys were always spoken to respectfully and this was noticed among all the other inmates, who then took their anger out on the favoured few. They were given a hard time, with name-calling and with many of the other inmates not having much to do with them.

One of these favoured boys was named Graeme. Sachisthal always gave him the good clean jobs and had Graeme in charge of the kitchen and dining room. Other inmates working under Graeme were treated badly by being reported on a daily basis for not performing duties properly or for very minor things like not wiping up or washing up in the perfect way in the rules laid down by Sachisthal. Sometimes plates were accidentally broken.

Whenever these minor things occurred, Graeme was out of the kitchen like a rabbit, knocking on the office door to report the boys. Next thing Sachisthal would appear and the boys who had been reported were punished, but not before Sachisthal had hit them across the head with a closed fist.

Generally, the punishment was that after the evening meal and having done their daily chores, they would be sent to the dining room to polish the wooden floors with wax, down on their knees for a few hours while everyone else was playing board games or doing homework. After everyone had gone to bed, except the boys on polishing duties, Sachisthal would inspect the work. If he was not satisfied, the boys would keep polishing until Sachisthal was satisfied; or if Sachisthal had gone to bed without warning they would be stuck in the dining room all night, without being able to go to bed. If the boys had gone to bed they would have been punished further.

Because the Home was always in urgent need of funds, Sachisthal would canvass many business people for assistance. He was seldom denied help. For example, many sellers and growers at the Haymarket fruit and vegetable markets would always have something to give to the Home. Once a week Mr Len Norman, who was an assistant officer to 'Sachie', would have three boys up early and off we would go to the markets in the Home's Fargo truck, which was a beige colour and had "Charlton Boys' Home" printed on both sides. Mr Norman with his English accent on arrival would send the boys off to the sellers we could rely on to have something for us. We often borrowed their equipment to take the donation back to the truck.

Without the help of these and other people, we would not have been so well fed. Australians are always the first to help anyone: that is the Australian way. Of course many market people came from other countries, but soon they were as 'Aussie' as anyone was. In broken English they would call out: "Over here mate, here's some bloody tomatoes." We would always say "Thank you very much" or "Please" because we had good manners. The Italians and Greeks were very good, hard-working people, many having come from war-torn Europe. They knew all about poverty and even though we were just "Home" kids, they were very respectful, as we were to them. Soon they were teaching us words, and they would laugh as we tried speaking their language. I often greeted them with hello in their own lingo, which would have them in screaming heaps of laughter over my mispronunciation or maybe they had deliberately taught me swear words. Nevertheless they were all good men trying to assist the Home.

Sachisthal had connections with Sydney Flour, which operated a small flourmill behind Grace Brothers on Broadway. We often picked up our 150-pound bags of flour and of porridge. Cameron Pie Factory, which started in Forest Lodge then later moved to the old AZ Bakery premises on Anzac Parade, Kensington, would nearly every week donate large numbers of pies, pasties and sausage rolls. All the inmates eagerly looked forward to these meals, served with mashed potatoes and other vegetables and, now and then, tomato sauce.

Miss Craig, the cook, had the help of Matron Emily Sachisthal. We always addressed her as Matron. Mrs Campbell would also lend a hand. Both were truly nice people and appeared to enjoy their work with all the boys. They were not easily fooled by anyone trying to put it over them: should a boy try it on, he did so at his own peril. Miss Craig was a large lady; she was very kind to all the boys and would often give you an extra biscuit or a piece of cake. God bless her for her kindness. She was a reasonable cook. Creamed celery soup was one of her special treats. Sadly she cooked cabbage to a mash, boiling out all the nutrients. She made nice custard and was a good woman: she always spoke kindly to all the boys.

9

The abuse

It was not often that Sachie would lose control of his actions, but I do recall a few times. When he was very angry, he would have all boys summoned to the Recreation Hall. I remember three occasions when I felt horrified as he lashed out at us, striking boys with his leather strap on the end of a long stick as he had us continuously running around the hall. This would go on for 30 minutes or so. In his anger he would lash out wildly, attempting to hit certain boys who he believed had misbehaved. Pity the poor innocent boys who got hit by mistake in the 'collateral damage' as we all attempted to dodge the leather whip. As he got tired his anger would drop, as well as the force in his lashing out. After a while he would line us up and give a speech telling us the reason we were all punished. Then he would dismiss us back to our chores.

There were two other occasions where very late in the evening on cold nights he would have all of us inmates lined up in the yard outside his office. Here he would keep us standing in the cold in only our nightwear as he scolded us. After standing in the cold he would have us run around the yard until he was satisfied we had suffered enough.

A few other times late at night he would have all of us out in the cold night where he had us all strip down in the nude. Here we stood for a long time. Then he would call out four boys at a time and they were ordered under the cold shower, where they stayed until he gave them permission to come out. "Get outside and wait," he'd scream out. We were not allowed towels to dry ourselves. Then he would call in four more boys and this went on until every boy had had a cold shower and been personally examined by Sachie, paying particular attention to each boy's penis. We stood in the cold, still wet, until he told us to pick up our nightwear and return to our beds. Shaking all over we could not dress until we reached our beds.

Whilst we were cold showering he watched us like a hawk, perving on us. He would call out loud to certain boys: "Are you still masturbating yourself every night?" "Come here," he would yell out, "let me check you over." Then he would examine the boy's penis. He would scream out: "I can tell by the redness of your penis that you've been masturbating tonight. Am I right? Have you been masturbating yourself tonight?" "No, Sir," the boy would say. "Yes you have," screamed Sachisthal, "and why are you telling me lies?"

He then turned to everyone else and said: "Hands up any boy who has been masturbating once a day, tell me the truth?" A few hands went up. "Tell me if you have been masturbating on a weekly basis?" A few more hands went up. Then he told these boys who had been masturbating to take a few steps back. Sachisthal then abused the boys who claimed they were not masturbating and screamed out they would be punished for not being truthful. The boys that would say yes to regular masturbation would be ordered to report to his office the next morning.

It is very important to point out here that this strange behaviour only happened when his wife Emily and Mrs Campbell were away from the home.

The next day, a few of my friends who were not in denial reported to Sachisthal's office after breakfast. All these boys stood in line outside his office. There were about a dozen boys, and they included Ken, David and Leonard. These three were my mates and they told me later that day what Sachisthal did to them. All three said the same thing, so we concluded he did the same checking of all the other boys that went into his office that morning. One at a time, they were ordered to fully undress alone in his office. Sachisthal told each of them that he was concerned they could have sexual diseases. Sachisthal then touched their private parts, looking closely as he felt them all over. When Sachisthal was satisfied they were disease-free, they were told to put their clothes on and to go back out and do their chores.

Ken was always in trouble because of his alleged nightly masturbation. At shower time before breakfast Sachie often called Ken out in front of everyone and screamed out that he would go insane if he didn't leave his penis alone. In hindsight I believe he tried to embarrass Ken, but I think he also got off by looking at Ken's rather large penis. Ken died during the 1990s and is buried near Batemans Bay.

I recall Sachisthal also asked every boy in turn if they were having sex with other boys, to which they all said no. Over the last few years, former inmates have told me that some boys in the Home were in fact having homosexual activities with each other. I never gave this much thought at the time, but I realise now that some boys were sexually assaulting younger boys. No doubt the old truism of violence leads to violence was very real at Charlton Boys' Home at Glebe.

Once Sachisthal called me out of the shower and examined my penis and embarrassed me by saying: "Carl, go see Ken Williams and have him show you how to masturbate – it's obvious that you seldom do it, because your penis is rather small." For a few days after this, a few of the boys including my mates asked how my masturbation was going. One thing for sure was I could take a joke from the boys. Often my reply was: "Better to have brains than a big penis."

Often Sachisthal took delight on cold mornings having all of us standing out in the cold court yard for long periods to a point we were all shivering. On a few occasions his mates Ray Menzies and Cecil Boyton would also perv on us having showers and afterwards while we waited in the nude for the order to dress.

If certain boys had upset him or he had it in for them, Sachisthal would give them double time and a longer inspection of their penis. In winter this punishment was so cruel. This extra cold shower time also caused them to be late for breakfast. "Why are you late?" he would scream out, making fun of them with remarks he thought were funny. He could be very facetious and make even the toughest boy feel small. How many of us wished we could instantly become invisible? More often than not he would punish them again by making them stand to eat breakfast and as a further punishment to make his point, he would send them to the kitchen to do extra duties.

By the time they were dismissed from the kitchen to get dressed for school they were late arrivals for school parade: perfectly planned by Sachisthal for him to repeat his sadistic, never-ending ritual. With every other boy standing in line waiting on their arrival, Sachisthal would scream out: "Why are you late?" They would stand silent, knowing Sachisthal was being facetious at their expense, and Sachisthal would order them to report to his office after they arrived home from school. They stood to attention outside his office whilst they awaited the further punishment. Sachisthal would arrive and tell them all previous punishments were inadequate and that they were to report at 6am the next morning for further cold showers. Of course some of the boys tried to apologise, which was very rarely accepted. Sachisthal could be very unreasonable if you got on his bad side.

I myself did not realise at that time that a few boys had absconded. Some just could not take it anymore. Those who ran away were not taken back and faced Court again, and those over 14 were sent to Mt Penang. Other younger boys finished up at Mittagong State Boys' Home, which had the reputation of being a very tough environment. A number of boys just gave up trying to be good: they went from bad to worse and finished up at that terrible prison called Tamworth. Most of us never realised for some time that boys had run away: the staff did their best to keep it secret.

I am so glad I was not a bed wetter, because these inmates would more often than not be punished by cold showers, washing their wet sheets along the way. Sometimes prior to cold shower punishment these inmates had to stand at the breakfast table to eat their breakfast, with their wet, urine-smelling sheets near them, which also punished inmates sitting near the smelling sheets. Unfortunately Sachisthal did not recognise that boys who wet the bed had terrible emotional problems. It was not like they wet the bed deliberately. It appears that people like Sachisthal just could not comprehend the emotional problems we brought with us.

Often of a night you would hear the mixed sounds through the quiet dormitory as boys masturbated, some boys much more than others. The sounds of a nightly ritual were rather mixed, with other boys sobbing as quietly as they could, some crying because of the constant sexual assaults by the many paedophiles within and outside the Home. I know now that in hindsight they were all friends of Norman Sachisthal.

Cold showers could be forced on boys late at night even when boys had been asleep. Sachisthal would drag them out of bed into the cold night for cold shower punishment.

Then there were the nightmares, which were always with us.

There were a few times when, getting up out of bed, every boy in both buildings was ordered to stand at the end of their unmade beds before going to the showers. Sachisthal personally inspected every boy's sheets. What was all this about, everyone was asking each other? Then the realisation came that he was checking to see if there were stains on the sheets and if boys were masturbating. And like the boys who urinated in their sleep, wetting the bed, any boy found having stains on his sheets was marched out for a cold shower and to wash his sheets under the cold shower.

There was a boy named Alan who was only about six years of age and who wet the bed nearly every night. One day Alan was being marched up to the shower block by Sachie for a cold shower and to wash his sheets. I thought it was wrong, so I said so to other inmates near me. I did not realise Sachisthal could hear what I said. Without warning he clipped the back of my head hard, then grabbed my ear and twisted it. He then proceeded to drag me along to the shower as well, saying out loud that I should mind my own business and keep my opinions to myself. This was my first cold shower punishment.

After this I kept my opinions within me: I was a fast learner. Sachisthal did not forget my intrusion into his methods of discipline and gave me bathroom cleaning duties; this included cleaning dirty toilets, where I had to make them as clean as possible every day for weeks. Having made his point very clearly and seeing I had repented, he relented, and I was back to normal chores. That was a lesson well learnt.

Later that year young Alan was in trouble again. At Sunday school the boy told his Sunday School teacher at St Barnabas Broadway how a part-time Charlton officer, Mr Joe Barnett, had raped him in the galvanised tin shed Barnett used to repair radios where often he taught a few boys how to repair them. Barnett worked full-time at AWA Radio at Ashfield in the repair department as well as being a part-time officer at Charlton. The teacher in turn told the minister at St Barnabas.

A few days after Alan reported this, all of us boys could hear shouting and screaming coming out of the superintendent's office where Alan had been hauled by Sachisthal to front his Sunday school teacher and the minister of St Barnabas. Everyone could hear Sachisthal defending his friend Joe Barnett and calling Alan a habitual liar and nothing but a troublemaker and soon the church people left not knowing the truth. After this Barnett had been given the "green light" to continue his paedophile conduct against Alan and other small children. Alan suffered punishment and humiliation at the hands of Sachisthal, as well as further sexual abuse and rape for the rest of his incarceration at Charlton.

During this period of Alan being raped, everyone knew about it and the boys spoke of it amongst themselves, secretly. This event and the consequences that Alan endured were the main reason during the 1950s why none of the boys, including me, would report their own sexual assaults.

My first really bad experience came from what I at first thought was goodness on Sachisthal's part. It was school holidays, and he chose about 20 boys to go on this Christmas camp down Camden way where there was a river nearby. The camp was called 'Toc H' and was a part of the YMCA, as were the many men who organised the camp. About 50 boys went, and every boy was enjoying something they had never been part of previously. Sporting activities were part of every day's recreation. We all participated in cross-country races and swimming races in the river. I was very good at most sports and won more races than I lost.

During this summer of 1950 it was very hot and after breakfast most of us would enjoy a few hours swimming in the river under supervision. There was a swinging rope attached to a large tree, which was real fun and we all took turns by lining up for our turn of the swinging rope. We then would return to our tents and line up in front of our tents for the daily inspection. Points were given each day for how tidy your tent was and how well your own space was kept.

The meals were ever so good. We even had eggs each day with our toast and even butter to spread. We had a choice of cereals and we poured Sunshine powdered milk over it and we could use as much sugar as we desired. The tea was better than at the Home and did not have that terrible bromide taste. Sometimes we even had bacon. At lunchtime we often had sandwiches and fruit and cakes to eat with our cup of tea. Our evening meals were really good with the usual vegetables around sausages and even steak and sometimes we had a mince stew. So we had real variety and there was always plenty left over for seconds.

But even the best things must end and what was good suddenly turned evil. One night in a sound sleep, I woke to strange things happening to me, and my pyjama pants down near my feet. I could not turn, as Mr Menzies who was beside me was holding me down and was hurting me badly, penetrating me. I tried very hard to push him away but he was stronger than I was. Once he was satisfied he got up off me, leaving me in pain and distress.

After he had left me, I noticed I was bleeding and there was cum all over me. I felt really dirty and I could not get back to sleep. I got up early before the sun started to rise, and I went by myself to the river to wash everything away. I was crying and very frightened by the bleeding from my backside. I had a short swim and arrived back to the tent as the others were getting dressed. I was the tent leader and checked my own gear was in order and checked all the other boys' gear. I was so ashamed of what Menzies did to me, I could not look anyone in the eyes. We all went to breakfast and there I saw Menzies again, who I avoided: I could not bring myself to look or speak to him. All day long I avoided him until just before bed that evening, when he cornered me and warned me about speaking to others of what he had done to me the previous night. There was no need to warn me: I hated him so much and wanted to report him, but I was too ashamed and was not going to tell a living soul.

That night I found it hard to sleep and I kept looking out of the tent as I was nearest the entrance. Soon everyone was asleep except me. I recall praying and asking my God to help me, over and over. I must have fallen to sleep because next thing I remember it was morning and one of the boys was shaking me awake.

The camp was over and we all packed and climbed on the back of the truck, which took about twenty of us, and then we were off on our return to the Home at Glebe. Sachisthal was waiting in the yard as we arrived home and told us to take our gear to our rooms and report back to his office. In the office was Ray Menzies laughing and joking with Sachisthal. After that Sachisthal told us what jobs we had to do. I wanted to tell him what happened, but because of the previous incident where little Alan Smith had reported being raped and was punished by Sachisthal ever after, I decided to keep my mouth shut and try and get over it. I could have told our dear friend Chaplain Ray Weir on his regular visits, but like other boys I chose to just keep quiet, mainly because I was too ashamed and because I knew I would be called a liar by Sachisthal and relentlessly punished thereafter.

I later discovered that Menzies had done the same thing to other boys during this camp. In hindsight I should have reported him to the police: I could have found a way if I had been brave enough, but I was a coward like all the other victims.

Soon the school holidays were over and we went back to school, starting a New Year by repeating first year at Glebe Technical School. I kept myself under the radar and always did what I was told and never complained. I trained and played in the Home's footy team, which was a terrible team: we never won a game.

One day early in the new year, Sachisthal called me to his office and asked Terry Matherson and me to go with a Mr Cecil Boyton to paint a house at Rouse Hill which belonged to a lady from the Church. We worked hard all day but could not finish the outside as darkness came too quickly. Boyton drove us back to the Home and told me he was picking me up early next day. I was waiting alone when he arrived: he only needed one boy to finish off.

After an enjoyable drive we arrived and with much energy I painted the house. Then I had to paint the windows and doors, which was slow work. I finished the whole job just as the sun was going down. The lady had a baked meal ready and served it after I washed up. I still recall the baked roast, which was surrounded by baked spuds and pumpkin and green peas and covered in gravy.

After the meal it was dark. Boyton had the Morris car started for the return trip. On the way back to Charlton he was showing me how to change gears. After about half an hour he pulled over and stopped in a secluded area. He came around to my side of the car and when he undid his trousers I instantly knew I was in big trouble.

He pulled me over to him, undid my buttons and started to fondle me. Then he was on his knees, giving me oral sex. After some time he made me masturbate him. He tried to make me give him oral sex, which I refused to do. This made him angry and he quickly pulled his trousers up and started the car. He drove quite fast and left me at the Charlton gate, with a warning to keep quiet or else.

It appears Boyton told Sachisthal that I was a good worker and this pleased Sachisthal, who praised me. Some days later he said that as a reward Boyton wanted to take me on a road trip and then spend the weekend at his Bundock Street, Randwick, home.

What could I do? I felt trapped. As I suspected, on the road trip south he soon found a secluded place to park out of the way of the public. He started by placing his hand on my penis. He then gave me oral sex, which seemed to last for a long time. Whilst this was going on he had me masturbate him with this oil that he took from a jar all over his penis. After some time he tried to force my mouth over his large penis, which I resisted and pulled away from his hold on me. Soon we were driving again and he stopped for a few drinks at a shop on the Windsor Road, then he drove back to his home at Randwick.

I was surprised that there were some other former Home boys living in his house. I recall after a meal everyone sat around the lounge room listening to the radio and as the night went on everyone went to bed. I fell asleep and during the night I woke to Boyton masturbating me from behind then penetrating me and hurting me so much. After what seemed like hours he got up and kissed me and then left.

I spent the following day talking to the other boys who had turned up. They were not surprised by what I told them about Boyton. I thought I was warning them, but they knew already.

That night Boyton returned me to the Home and after speaking to Sachisthal he drove off.

Over the coming months, Boyton often asked for me to go to his house or to go to other places and he would always try the same thing over and over, but after a while he got the message I did not like what he was up to. Eventually he stopped asking for me and started taking other innocent and very gullible boys out. I never asked them what happened, but it was obvious to me they were all being sexually molested and raped as I had been.

There were a few other paedophiles taking boys out and I was always pleased when they did not ask me to go.

One place I loved going to was Mr and Mrs Blacket's home at Harbord. I went there on and off and did gardening, painting or any other odd jobs needing attention. I used to love the tram and then the Manly ferry trip and bus to Harbord: it made for a really pleasant day. The Blackets were the nicest people I worked for. They would put my pay in a sealed envelope as requested by Sachisthal. They knew I could not touch this money so on the side they would give me ten shillings to spend that Sachisthal knew nothing about. I recall one Sunday Mr Blacket rang Sachie for permission for me to stay over, as they wanted to take me to a special Church Service at their Harbord Church of England Church where the Rector – a Reverend Rogerson who had come from Holy Trinity at Erskineville – was a blind man.

At mealtime, they would always say grace. On my birthday they gave me my first Bible. I still have this King James Holy Bible. I have always treasured it, because they gave it to me and with it came their love. Mr Blacket wrote a verse in my Bible from the Corinthians One, Chapter 13, Verse 13: "And now abideth Faith, Hope and Charity, these three, but the greatest of these is Charity." One day this Bible will pass to one of my children. I hope they cherish it as I have. It brings back many good memories that have always remained with me.

Mrs Blacket once said she would have loved to have had a son like me.

After a while unfortunately there was no more work to do and I was no longer needed. For a while nobody asked to take me out, which suited me fine. I devoted much of my time to working around the Home putting down brick paved paths and assisting Mr Hardy, the plumber, put a new galvanised roof on the long single storey building which became the new gym and double garage area for the vehicles. I also worked on the new 15 feet high retaining walls.

After turning 15 in June 1952, Sachisthal suggested I leave school and said I had to pay my own way. I left school and my full-time working life began. I have often regretted not going further with my schooling: if my life had been more normal, I might have had an opportunity to even go to university. But Sachisthal wanted me working as soon as possible so as to pay my board. He often embarrassed boys who did not pay.

Before long he had secured a full-time job for me with Cameron's Pie Factory, which was on Anzac Parade, Kensington. It soon became obvious that the owner, Mr Alex Whitson, was another paedophile who was relentless in molesting the Home boys. He also was a good friend of Sachisthal. Whitson was rather well off, lived with his sister at Randwick and owned a weekend cottage near Whale Beach. Here he often took Home boys away for dirty weekends.

It was not long before I saw Whitson molesting one of the boys in his office. I was outside stacking boxes against the walls and saw everything. Often I would walk in and catch him masturbating and he would just carry on regardless. Mick Campbell warned me not to get caught alone with him.

I later discovered that no Home boy ever escaped Whitson's attention. After a while he used to keep me back with extra work and, going in to get your pay after everyone had gone, you would find him sitting at his desk masturbating. Unperturbed, he would pull you near him as you tried to sign for your pay. He would fondle you whilst masturbating and then he would go down on your penis, giving you oral sex. He would force you to hold his penis and try to force you to also give him oral sex, which I never would and this annoyed him. Once he tried unsuccessfully to rape me whilst I was stacking 150-pound bags of flour. I told him I would report him but he just laughed at me, saying I wouldn't be believed. He penetrated me and his penis was so large he hurt me as he tried his best for full penetration. But with me fighting him off violently he soon lost the urge to rape me and gave up. This was a great victory for me.

I got even with Whitson. Most days he had me bring him a cup of tea into his office. One day I had the bright idea to urinate into his cup of tea. I did this often when I had the opportunity. He must have liked the added urine because he never complained.

I think Whitson knew no boy would take the chance to report him to Sachisthal. This was because he donated hundreds of pies and pastries a few times a week to the Home and we knew Sachisthal liked him very much. Over the last few years about 20-odd boys have told me how he raped or molested them, often at his weekender up near Whale Beach. To my knowledge he was never reported.

10

Role of Sachisthal

In 2004 I placed a submission before the "Forgotten Australians" Senate Hearings in Canberra. My submission was about the paedophiles who had hurt me so badly as a teenager. By 2006 I began to advertise for contact with other former Charlton boys, with a view to organising a reunion. So many former inmates related to me in confidence allegations of how they were sexually violated by paedophiles. Just a few of their stories are in Appendix One.

These allegations by many former inmates were against Sachisthal, Raymond Bruce Menzies, Cecil Boyton, Alexander Whitson, Bob Davies, Ted Lord, Joe Barnett, Albert Ables, Mr Schell and others. Sexual allegations were also made in separate submissions against officers at other Charlton Homes such as Ashfield, Bowral and Castle Hill. The allegations were that senior staff were either involved directly, or knew what was going on and did nothing.

All these people had associations with young boys like me by being employed by the Church of England or by being friends of the Homes and trusted by superintendents such as Sachisthal. For a while, I thought Sachisthal was just gullible, but after talking to many other inmates I now know better. Ron Nichols convinced me first of what Sachisthal was really like, and then many others afterwards made similar allegations of being sexually abused by Sachisthal himself. Ron Nichols, who later changed his name to Ron West, had his arm and leg broken during one of Sachisthal's violent sexual assaults. According to Ron, they did not seek hospital attention until the next day. Ron was warned about speaking out against Sachisthal and like others he kept quiet, saying that he had had a bad fall.

During the last ten years, I have spoken to hundreds of former Charlton Glebe inmates who believe Sachisthal and other staff were never concerned about them when they left the home. They believe they were sent out alone with no follow up help. Many ended up in gaol or on drugs or in drunken relationships filled with violence. Many of these former inmates had life-long mental problems and were badly in need of psychological assistance. There were many that could not take the daily pain and memories, and committed suicide.

What really makes my blood boil is that Sachisthal was considered a really good man who did a lot for boys in his care. I have dozens of newspaper clippings from the 1960s stating what a "great man" he was. These are just two of them:

Daily Telegraph, **Thursday May 22, 1961: "Half a Century of Helping Delinquents"**
For almost 21 years the Sachisthals ran the Charlton Boys' Home at Glebe. Mr Sachisthal was Superintendent and his wife Matron. "I loved every minute of my life there. We were just one big happy family," Mr Sachisthal recalled ...
"With the right atmosphere, plenty of love, team spirit and discipline, we felt we could make a decent citizen of any of the boys sent to us," he said.
It is this love of children that has ensured their complete devotion over the years.

Sunday Telegraph, March 12, 1961: "No Locks, No Warders … and Never a Riot!"
The Child Welfare Department has a high regard for Charlton … officials send a troublesome inmate to 'Sachy' to see whether he can win over the boy – and, more often than not, he does.
Much of the answer to this is with 'Sachy' himself- the personification of just about any boy's image of a good father. At times gruff, stern, even ready to "clip a young villain's ear", Mr Sachisthal is also a man with a big heart and a sympathetic understanding bolstered by a sound religious spirit and his own years as a father. He has made Charlton much more of a home than a Home …

Sachisthal was awarded the OBE in 1961 for his "services to child welfare". This is the citation that went with his award:

HONOURS AND AWARDS 10TH JUNE 1961
Appointed a member of the civil division of the most excellent order of the British Empire.
NORMAN ALBERT SACHISTHAL ESQUIRE
CITATION
FOR SERVICES TO CHILD WELFARE
Mr Sachisthal is Superintendent of the Charlton Memorial Home for Boys, which he founded in 1942. This Home, which is an agency of Church of England Social Services, provides accommodation for boys whose home circumstances are unfavourable or who have appeared before Children's Courts.
Mr Sachisthal's dedication, conviction and sympathy, coupled with long years of tedious and frequently unrewarding work, have made the Home a success and have been responsible for the rehabilitation of hundreds of boys.

How this award could ever have been granted is still a mystery to me.

11

Returning home

With a month to go before I could leave Charlton, I became very frustrated as the days seemed longer and went past so slow. As each day passed, I marked it off on my calendar. Soon there were only five days to go and they could not arrive fast enough: Monday, then Tuesday and soon it was Friday 26 June 1953, my sixteenth birthday and my last day at Charlton.

As soon as I arrived back at Charlton from work, I walked into Sachisthal's office and said: "Sir, this is my last day". I did not give him my pay as I did not want him taking more from me. Sachisthal said: " I haven't worked out yet what money is due to you. I'll fix it up and have it ready early Saturday morning. Get packed and after breakfast you are free to leave."

The next morning I was waiting outside his office after breakfast. Sachisthal soon arrived, gave me a sealed envelope and wished me luck. I then told him what Whitson had been doing to me and other boys at the pie factory. His response was totally dismissive: "I don't think so. You're just trying to make trouble."

With my few belongings packed, I made my way back to

Erskineville. I never did go back to see anybody at Charlton. I had no reason to.

I returned to Erskineville a very angry teenager, to live with my mother and new stepfather. The sexual molestation I had endured silently, telling nobody, had taken away any happiness I had and the light was missing from my eyes. I had no faith in my mother: she had hurt me so much throughout my life. What good would it do me to tell her of the three years of sexual assaults? I made up my mind to try and forget about the abuse. But try as I may, it remained in my thoughts to haunt me.

Over the next few weeks I found a job as a Dispatch Clerk with Stromberg Carlson Radio, a radio manufacturing company which was situated on Bourke Street, Alexandria. I went back to Cameron's Pie Factory and gave Whitson a week's notice. Even on my last day he still tried to molest me by massaging me. I remember calling him a dirty stinking poofter and telling him I was going to tell the police. But I didn't: I was still too embarrassed and ashamed.

I told some of my best mates about Whitson and what had happened to me. It was because of my bad experiences with paedophiles that my friends and I despised homosexuals. I thought for a long time that homosexuals and paedophiles were the same thing. So one night a group of us decided to go to Kings Cross with the intention of picking a fight with a homosexual. That proved easy to do: while we were enjoying ourselves, a homosexual put the hard word on one of my mates, who then bashed him up.

We went back to the Cross a number of times looking to bash homosexuals. We would bait them and then pick fights with them. It was always one-on-one: we never ganged up on them and we fought clean. If the homosexual was hurt and couldn't get up, we would help them up and then walk away.

This behaviour, of which I am not proud, lasted a few years until my National Service.

BABY IAN

When I first returned to our house at Albert Street Erskineville, Mum and Vic had gone to live with Vic's mother for a while while Mum was pregnant with Ian and then for the delivery. During this period, my mates and I had plenty of parties at Albert Street. Alan Forrest, who was a few years older than us and worked with a lot of girls at a factory in Alexandria, often brought girls much older than us to our house and we would party on over the weekend with lots of sex. They were all beautiful girls and very sexy.

Some of the neighbours eventually called the police, telling them we were running a brothel. The police came and spoke to me, and I told them we were only having parties, the girls were our girlfriends and there were no prostitutes at any of our parties.

Mum allowed the rent to fall behind at Albert Street and so we had to move. Mum had what little furniture there was transported to 14 Gladstone Street in Balmain East, next door to the Pacific Hotel. Mum could not have chosen a better place, considering how much she loved her beer.

The house had three rooms downstairs with two bedrooms upstairs. I was working at Alexandria and rode my bike back and forth five days a week, rain or shine.

Balmain was a very old suburb and at this time a true working man's suburb, unlike today where it is full of many who believe they are better than others are. In these early days, Balmain was a true industrial area and claimed to have a pub on near every corner. Neville left Carlingford and came to live with us for a short while before we moved again.

While we lived at Gladstone Street, Vic and Mum put a small deposit on a very old weatherboard cottage in Waterview Street.

Sometimes I had to go around to collect the rent. But they lost the house soon after, being unable to repay the loan.

One Saturday at Gladstone Street, while Vic was working overtime, Mum had me running back and forth to the hotel next door getting her jug filled with beer, just like she used to do. She was in no state to look after Ian, who was just a little baby. Well, Mum fell asleep and I could here the baby crying. It was never-ending, so I opened the door to Mum's bedroom. The smell was terrible: Mum had vomited all over the floor and bedding and Ian was in urgent need of a change of napkins. I didn't know what to do, so I just closed the door and went downstairs.

Soon afterwards, Vic walked in and asked where Mum was. I said she was asleep. The baby was still crying and Vic walked up the stairs. I could hear them screaming abuse at each other. Then Vic asked me if I had got any grog next door for Mum. I told him she had had me going back and forth all morning. Vic went upstairs and the fighting continued, then Mum in a loud drunken voice told Vic that the vomit all over the room was from the baby. She must have thought Vic was an idiot. Vic said: "What, has the baby been drinking beer all day, because the vomit has a strong beer smell!"

He told Mum she should be ashamed of herself and if she did not wake up to herself he was leaving.

I had been out of Charlton less than one year, and here I was again back in the same hellhole. I was truly sick of all the drinking which always resulted in brawls. Sometimes Mum would go missing up Balmain way and leave me minding the baby.

LIVING WITH ABORIGINES

After we had been at Balmain for just over one year, Mum was given money by the landlord to move because he wanted to sell the house with vacant possession. Vic and Mum rented an old two-story house at 150 Botany Street, Waterloo. Our backyard faced the rear of the picture theatre on Botany Road. It seemed to me we were going backwards in regards to where we lived. Waterloo did not have a good name, because of the myriad of alcoholic Aboriginal people living in the district.

I was still working at Strombergs, which was good work but the money was not very good. I knew I would soon need to look for another job with better money if I was going to advance myself at all. But soon the decision was taken for me: after the yearly Christmas party, many of us were advised by a note in our pay envelope that our services were no longer required. I could stay on after Christmas if I would consider working machinery in the factory. This did not appeal to me, as the wages would remain the same with no chance of advancement.

I did not like Waterloo at all. We were right in the centre of hundreds of Aboriginal families. You had to live near these people to truly understand how they lived. Many of them were drunk, very dirty-looking and unhygienic. But they never bothered us or caused us any trouble. In fact I found most of them very friendly and always said hello. I treat people as they treat me and I always reciprocated by being friendly. This was in the 1950s and all of us knew the Aboriginal people had never been given a fair go since white people arrived in 1788. I always believed that all governments just hoped the black problem would go away.

The Waterloo hovels where the Aborigines lived were badly run down and always very messy, with food and bottles thrown all around the area among other disgusting body waste. Old broken furniture was in heaps along the footpaths. Many houses had no front doors and most had broken windows. If you walked past some Aboriginal houses you would be gasping for breath because the smell was enough to make you vomit.

Little Aboriginal children roamed the street in the nude or

with very little clothing. Often they had no underwear and never any shoes. If I had a bag of sweets that I'd bought coming home from work and felt sorry for them I would give them the bag of sweets to share. They did not have much but nevertheless they were always laughing and happy. I have often wondered how life treated these poor Aboriginal kids as they grew up.

In and around Botany Street it was all too common to see these people arguing and fighting violently and often these fights would go on all day. The women would throw drunken men out of the houses and the men would sleep off the demon drink on the footpaths.

I learned quickly to walk past or around them and to never make any comments. The whole idea was to make out you didn't notice them while at the same time minding your own business. There were times I had two or three young drunken Aborigines approaching me and if you continued straight towards them, sure enough they would try to pick a fight with you. Other times they would only be after a few shillings as they tried to bludge on you. To avoid problems, I sometimes found it was wiser to just cross the street.

There were a number of hotels on Botany Road and you would see many Aborigines fighting as they were thrown out of the hotels. Sometimes they were violent, all-in brawls and people would have blood streaming from their wounds and in a short time the police would arrive and bundle them into the police wagons. The badly injured were ferried by ambulances to Prince Alfred on Missenden Road, Camperdown, which was always a busy hospital.

I hated Waterloo. Why on earth would Vic and Mum have chosen to live in such a dump? I'll never know. Waterloo was a filthy, unhygienic area and I now understand why Aboriginal children and adults have a high death rate.

MEN'S WAGES FOR MEN'S WORK

While living at Waterloo, Mum was not happy with the wages I was getting at Stromberg Carlson of £6 a week, of which she took £4. When I lost my job at Strombergs she had me go and see a friend of hers – a Mr Frank Murphy, who was the Manager of Crago Flour Mill which was located adjacent to the Newtown railway station and from here the wheat trains would unload their wagons of wheat. All our wheat came from country NSW. Crago also had flour mills elsewhere in country NSW.

Well Frank Murphy gave me a job on trial and said if I could do a man's work he'd pay me a man's wage. I was not going to fail: within a few days I could hand-sew the bags of semolina and keep up with the voluminous supply of semolina to be bagged and sewn and wheeled away to the storeroom.

My wages were £13.10.0 per week on day shift of forty hours. There was also plenty of extra work, and most weeks I earned around £25. But with me getting £13 plus at the flour mill, Mum raised my board to £10 a week. I eventually woke up to myself: with Mum being so greedy I never told her about the extra overtime pay.

Anyone who has ever worked in a large flour mill will testify that it was very hard physical work. But I loved it and it also kept me very fit. After a few weeks I became roller boy, which saw me in charge of the rollers. A month later I was sent to pack flour from the flour press machines, which was harder. Each bag had to have at least ten stitches and twice around each ear. With around ninety-five 140-pound bags per hour, you had to be fast.

Later I was made rollerman and then eventually topman, which had me in charge of the four flowmasters who separated the crushed wheat as it rotated around the mill, eventually becoming flour, semolina, wheat germ, bran and pollard. The topman job required constant observation of the flowmasters. I loved the job and the extra money, which had me on £16.0.0 per week.

Through all the overtime, which I never knocked back, I saved enough money to buy a three-in-one radio with record player and a tape recorder. Later I bought Mum a new bedroom suite, because she told me she needed a new one and I could afford such a gift.

Soon we were very busy at the mill: we were getting all these government orders under the 'Colombo Plan', which was flour and other products donated as foreign aid to Asian countries.

We were now working the mill seven days a week and 24 hours a day. I always remember once going to work at seven o'clock Monday morning and not finishing until three o'clock the following Saturday afternoon. When the mill was running problem free, the shift millers would tell me to catch a few hours sleep on the packed bags of flour. After a sleep here and there I would have a shower to refresh myself for another 16 hours or more before a further break. This work extended over many months and often I did up to three double shifts each week.

I never let on to Mum how much extra I was earning. With the money I saved I bought myself a 125 cc CZ motorbike. I loved this bike and it made my getting to and from work very quick.

I talked Frank Murphy into giving my brother Neville a job at Crago's. Frank said: "Carl, if he's as good as you, I'll pay him men's wages". I had previously got Neville a job in a hat factory on Wilson Street, Newtown. Neville started at seven one morning and walked out just after lunch the same day: they had him take the morning tea and lunch orders, and not being able to read or write he stuffed up all the orders. Everyone was going crook on him, so Neville just walked out the door, never to be seen there again.

Within a week at Crago's, Neville was sewing the semolina bags of 150 pounds really well. Mr Murphy told Neville he was on men's wages. Each month we had to pay our union fees to an old-grey haired bloke who was the Mill Union Delegate. The union motto was: "What you eat today walks and talks tomorrow." Unionism was compulsory: no card, no job.

I had a few mates at work. One was Morton Sutherland and his cousin Johnny Sutherland. On weekends we often used go to town. Morton was a very good country singer and he played his guitar well. We once went to Howard Craven's Rumpus Room. This was an afternoon young people's show and was on Radio 2UE. Morton was invited to sing and as usual sang a Hank Williams song.

Morton used to entertain us at work and on weekends would use my tape recorder to record his music. It did not take long before all the boys at Crago's called him Tex Morton. Through Tex we were invited to many parties. Girls were plentiful. We often went to Luna Park to pick up girls or sometimes we took our own girls.

12

My first motor car and the deadly accident

Tex and I bought an old 1927 Chrysler touring car with a canvas roof and canvas windows. An older guy who lived near Tex's parents at Engadine sold it to us for £10. It used a lot of oil and required constant top-ups.

All the next weekend we drove the car around. We took the same streets over and over as we all took turns driving. While driving the old car along Noble Avenue near Chiswick Street I hit a very big pothole, which made the car impossible to steer. As I tried to straighten the car, the steering wheel came away and was in my hands. We were heading for a telegraph pole, out of control, then bang into the pole. All the electric wires came down and there were sparks everywhere. Ever so carefully we got ourselves out of the car and looked around at the damage, but our main concern was the live wires.

We decided that Johnny Sutherland would stay with the car and make sure nobody came near the live wires. Tex and I went searching for a phone box to call the police. We found two phones but they were out of order, so we decided to go to the Police Box at Punchbowl, which was empty when we arrived there. Then having rung the police we made tracks back to the accident site. By the time we got back, the police, an ambulance and the Electric Light Company were already there, and there was a big crowd. John saw us and told us a little boy had walked onto the wires and had been electrocuted.

We saw the ambulance taking the poor little boy away. We were told later that his name was Graham Collins and he was only seven years old. I saw a lady running up and she was crying: she was the little boy's mother and obviously she had been told about her boy. My mates and I were in great shock and this became worse when the policeman told us the little boy was in a critical condition.

I told the policeman what happened. He took photographs of the car, the pole and the large pothole. The authorities also went along Noble Avenue taking photographs of rolled up electric wire sitting on top of the telegraph poles. We found out later that when the electricity men had finished work on the Friday, they had rolled up the wire and left them live. When our car hit the pole, the live electric wires came tumbling down.

That afternoon all three of us met the policeman at the Punchbowl Police Box and made statements. The Officer asked Johnny a few questions and realised why Johnny was left behind. The police asked John: "Why did you not stop the little boy going near the live wires?" Johnny said he saw a dog walk over the wires and nothing happened, so he thought maybe someone had turned the power off and so had no further concerns.

The policeman then told us the little boy had died on the way to hospital. We were so shocked none of us could contain our emotions. We had started the day just trying to learn to drive and never imagined the day would end so badly with an innocent little boy being electrocuted.

I felt weak and sick and vomited outside the Police Box. I kept repeating: "Why me? How could this have happened?" Then when I calmed down I apologised to the policeman for thinking about myself: I realised that the dead little boy's family were suffering much more than me. After a while the three of us were more composed as we answered questions that the policeman required answers to. He was very critical of Johnny Sutherland and told him he should have used more common sense.

I asked the policeman whether we could see the parents and try to explain what happened. He said yes but not today and suggested we leave it to later during the week. He gave us the Chiswick Street address.

A few days later all three of us were knocking on the Collins family's front door. A man answered the door and we told him who we were. We were so nervous and very anxious and thought we would be abused: God only knows we deserved to be. We were invited into the lounge room. Mrs Collins was still in tears as she sat down. We all took turns telling her everything we knew and all of us were crying as we tried to say how sorry we were. At last Mrs Collins said: "I would like to talk to you, but I can't find the words." She said the policeman had spoken to her about us and she appreciated we cared enough to see her. The man could see it was hard on Mrs Collins and told us to come back later when things were calmer. He saw us to the door and he told us that the Electricity Company had a lot to answer for, because they had no right to leave live wires bundled up on top of the telegraph poles. He told us that the policeman had said this would all be brought up at the Coroner's hearing.

We spoke about going to the funeral and we thought maybe it would be better if we just sent a floral arrangement and a sympathy card. A few months later I wrote a letter to Mrs Collins, hoping this might help her in her sorrow.

We had to face up to our own stupidity, driving such an old car even though it was registered. I have no idea how many times I asked God to forgive me.

We had a scrap dealer pick up the car and were paid a small amount for it. We decided to go to the Post Office and get a money order and send it to Mrs Collins, hoping it would assist her with funeral costs.

After leaving my mates on that terrible day, I went home to Waterloo. It was around 5pm and I went upstairs to where Vic and Mum were still in bed. With full detail I told them how a little boy had died. Mum did not allow me to finish my story. She called me a murderer and said I should be in gaol. I realised nothing would be gained by trying to make her fully informed as to who was really at fault. Vic and Mum were both drunk in bed. I tried to explain things to them, but Mum just kept saying I should be ashamed to murder a little boy on her birthday.

Without a doubt this was the most horrible day of my life and a day that would remain ingrained in my memory all my life. In my mother's eyes I was a murderer. Nobody could imagine how much this hurt me and worse still I had no other family support. For the next few years I often had bad dreams as I could not erase it from my mind.

Later I received a notice to attend the Burwood Coroner's Court again and with the boy's family in attendance. The Coroner found that the Electricity Company and their staff were negligent and were responsible for Graham Paul Collins being electrocuted and his ultimate death. Bankstown Council was criticised for not keeping secondary roads in better repair. The Coroner said that I was not at fault. The case closed and the Punchbowl policeman came over and wished me the best of luck.

As soon as I returned home I told Mum the Coroner's verdict.

I demanded an unconditional apology, which put her back on her heels. "How dare you speak to me in that tone of voice?" she yelled. I told her she was too stubborn and was incapable of saying sorry. I walked out, telling her to have another drink of the Tolleys Brandy hidden in the laundry where it would not be found by Vic.

Even though she knew that it was an accident and that the Coroner had found me blameless, Mum still continued to call me a murderer. She never let up. Mum was truly a malicious person and found great delight in upsetting and hurting my feelings.

The terrible events of that day still come back to my mind in great detail, especially every 29 January, as this was the day it happened and is also my mother's birthday.

MUM PRETENDS TO GAS HERSELF

One day it had been very hot at the flourmill and I knocked off at 3pm as the next shift came on. They were in for a great surprise, because during the day we had caught at least 100 pigeons on the main roof. By we, I mean my good mate Wally Cheal, who was the smutterman on my shift, and me. Our trap was a six-foot by eight-foot wire cage, which we placed plenty of wheat under. As soon as we had lots of birds under the cage, we would pull the rope and the cage dropped, catching the birds. We put them in large sacks and put them in Wally's car, except for about 20 or so. These birds we placed in the lockers of the afternoon shift, who were due to change clothes ready for work.

All the men were shocked as they opened their lockers and had birds flying out and around the change room and shower section. "Who put these bloody pigeons in our lockers?" they asked. They were all having a guess until they spotted Wally and me laughing our heads off. "You silly bastards," said Snowy, "you could have given me a heart attack." Tom Radley heard all the noise and came in to investigate. When all the pigeons were released in the open, he turned to Wally and me, trying to hide his laughter, and chastised both of us. Wally fattened the birds up and his wife Ellen baked them. Often Wally could be seen having baked pigeon in his meal break.

One Friday afternoon, to get away from Mum, I suggested to her that Neville and I would take little Ian to the pictures on Botany Road. These premises backed right onto our back yard. Vic was working the afternoon shift this Friday; he now worked for the Colonial Sugar Company at Pyrmont.

We wandered around to the theatre. It was a real bughouse. In those days they showed two movies and always began with cartoons. After the first movie they had interval and we would buy Fantales or Minties but mostly packets of Smiths chips and a Coke, Pepsi or Canada Dry.

After the movies were over we went straight home, which was only a few minutes walk. We knocked on the front door for 10 minutes and with no answer we just sat down on the verandah. After a while we looked under the mat and found the key.

We turned the front room light on and walked through to the kitchen. To our horror, there was our mother lying on the floor with her head on a towel poked into the bottom of the gas oven.

Neville was the first to wise up to the fact that the gas had not been switched on. Mum often did theatrical things like this to get everyone's attention and sympathy, but this time Mum had outdone herself: this was the most dramatic performance she had ever pulled. I realised Mum was acting and said to Neville: "Looks as if Mum's killed herself while we were out," and winking at Neville I said: "Watch Ian while I go out and call the police." Neville, by now sick and tired of Mum's rubbish, replied: "She can't be dead Carl because she forgot to turn the gas on."

Suddenly Mum jumped up and called us all the foulest

language you've ever heard. She then started to throw pots and pans and everything in her reach. A pan hit Neville and he jumped onto the top of the stove and up into the loft to get out of the way. As I tried to get around her in the very small kitchen, she hit me on the head with her frying pan. Neville up in the loft was calling out to me: "Carl, get out: the bloody drunken maniac will kill you."

I managed to get past her, but in doing so copped a myriad of blows to my face and head. I ran out the door and kept walking right up to Erskineville, to my mate Dave DeBelin's place where I stayed the night. I returned home on Sunday when Mum had quietened down. I went straight to the bedroom that I shared with Neville and we spoke about what had happened.

"I don't know what you intend doing Carl, but I'm getting out of this rat house," Neville said. He said he had spoken to Mrs Hatton up in George Street, Redfern. "I told her what a crook life we were having with Mum," Neville said. "Mrs Hatton offered me a room. Do you want to come with me Carl?"

I said I wasn't sure what to do. Mrs Hatton's son George was the Yasmar officer who had attacked me in Charlton when I was 13. I had heard a number of stories about his behaviour towards the boys after he moved to Carlingford Boys' Home. I attempted to be tactful with Neville, asking him if he was ever interfered with by Hatton. I never received a reply: it was as if Neville were saying, "Keep out of this."

Neville begged me not to tell Mum where he was going to live. I promised him I would keep it to myself.

On the Monday I went to work at Crago's, but Neville did not show up for work. I told Frank Murphy that Neville was sick, which was really not a lie because emotionally Neville could not cope with Mum's behaviour. That day Neville had got all his things together and packed, and as soon as Mum went down the backyard he grabbed his things and quickly left by the front door. When I arrived home from work that afternoon, Mum wanted to know if I had seen Neville. I told her no. I went upstairs and came down a few minutes later and asked her what had happened to all of Neville's things. This was done to protect myself and not to be blamed for Neville's quick departure.

She immediately flew up the stairs and I could hear her swearing her head off, so to keep away from her, I went up the back yard and played with Dolly, our dark brown and white spotted fox terrier.

For weeks Mum carried on about Neville, asking me if I saw him at work and did I know where he was living. I would answer, "yes he is still at work" and "no I have no idea because he won't tell me because he knows I'll tell you". This appeared to have convinced her that I knew nothing. But to make it more convincing I said: "He never wants to see you again." The shock of what I told her caught her by surprise and new foul words spewed from her foul mouth.

After a while she ceased to ask me about Neville, except one day when she said my board would have to go up to make up for the money Neville use to pay her for board. I said to her: "What do you expect from me? You're already taking £10 from my £13: don't you know what fair means?" I said if that was not good enough I would leave as well. Mum did not know what to say.

I often saw Neville. We loved riding our pushbikes everywhere and we often rode to Coogee Beach and other places around Sydney. I never spoke to Mum about being with Neville. Neville returned to work at Crago's for a while but then suddenly stopped. When I made inquiries I discovered he had also left his accommodation at Mrs Hatton's place. I lost contact with him for a long time after that. He was only 15.

13

On the move again

Neville had been gone some time now and I was still living with Mum at Waterloo, which was a slum of a place. Things were not getting any better with Mum. One day she told me we would soon be moving again, as the owners wanted to sell the property with vacant possession. Mum was given money for expenses connected with moving and within weeks everything was finalised and we moved to Rochford Street, Erskineville.

The house was a single storey dirty-looking terrace house with a shared lane separating the houses. The frontage was 24 feet wide and went back a little over 100 feet to the back fence. The front verandah was just wide enough for a single bed. This was where I slept. It was near impossible to make your bed: to get in or out of the room you had to walk over the bed. My clothes had nowhere to go; I can't recall where I kept them.

As you walked in the house, the first room was used as a lounge room, which was where Ian slept on an old settee. Along the hallway to the left was Mum and Vic's room, then came the small kitchen, then a door leading out to the back yard. Adjacent to the kitchen was an old lean-to corrugated tin laundry, which had washing tubs and an old galvanised bath. Outside was a gate to the shared laneway. The toilet was way down near the back fence. I had what I reckon was the smallest bedroom in Australia: about 12 feet long by three feet wide.

Within just a few years, our travels had taken us in one huge circle from Erskineville to Balmain East to Waterloo and back to Erskineville. With each move we appeared to be poorer and the houses got worse. The only good thing here was that it was much closer to work and also to all my old mates.

My old mates and I spent many leisure hours at football or other sports and sometimes having a quiet beer at the Rose of Australia Hotel in Erskineville, where we played cards. Sometimes I took girls out on dates. I always found the company of the gentle sex very good: they had a different way about them and they always made me very relaxed. Sometimes we would see a movie or just simply hang out. Most of my girlfriends loved having sex, no matter where: sometimes in the local parks, sometimes in their homes. During my stay here at Rochford Street I got to know a rather good-looking girl, Jean, who lived next door with the Carter family. Like me she had a verandah room, but it was twice the size of mine.

Jean seemed very lonely. Whenever she saw me she started a conversation. Often she would be waiting out the front of her house when I arrived home from work. We became real good friends and many times on a weekend night I would call in and see her and we would play cards for fun, with no betting. Afterwards she would kiss me passionately, giving me my first experience of French kissing with her tongue right down my throat. Honestly I did not like that style of kissing. Jean would get excited quickly and would take my shirt and trousers off before you could blink. Then she was on top of me, which lasted for ages.

As time went by, Jean became more and more amorous and would often call me to the back fence even if my mother was in the house. Here she would kiss me passionately and give me more French kisses. Jean was about four years older than I was. She often invited me into her bed and showed me things I had never even thought about before. Jean showed me all the different ways to enjoy each other's bodies and we had sex every way you could think of.

Jean told me of her tragic life. She never had family who loved her or who would give her a kiss or a cuddle and say: "I love you." Jean and I had a lot in common. Then she would say: "Enough of that: let's have some more sex." Jean was dynamite in bed. The only thing I would not participate in was anal sex and Jean told me it was not what she liked in any case.

I used to take Jean out a fair bit, mostly to the theatre and other places where we could enjoy each other's company, generally down in the rear double seats which were especially for lovers. If I was short of money she would not hesitate to pay. Sometimes we would go to a nice restaurant in town or around Enmore; if she ever paid I would make sure I paid her back on my payday. In my day I believe we had much more respect for the fairer sex and experienced or inexperienced young ladies, and I always showered them with all my attention and care.

My mother was a very jealous woman. When she saw I was very fond of Jean, Mum started putting Jean down, saying she was a prostitute and very low class. I thought to myself: Isn't this the pot calling the kettle black? I told Mum that Jean had never asked me for money and that in fact she often paid and would not allow me to repay her when I took her out to dinner or a show or to a dance.

It was not hard to see through my mother. She probably thought if things got too serious with Jean she would lose the goose who supplied her with the golden egg. She tried everything to persuade me to cut off our romance.

Sometimes when Jean and I had gone out somewhere, on my arrival back home I would find my mother had blockaded the front entrance to prevent me getting in to the house. When this happened I would return to see Jean, who would let me in to share her bed for the night. I spent many great nights with Jean thanks to Mum locking me out.

One day I came home from work and having not seen Jean for a few days I knocked on the Carters' front door. They told me Jean had left suddenly the day before after having spent all night with me. She left a message for me. It said she was so sorry to leave but she knew that there were too many obstacles for us to have a permanent relationship, especially my mother who the previous day had abused hell out of her after she had got so mad with my mother's behaviour and said to her: "You're only jealous because you want Carl to give you sex." Jean said she loved me more than anyone else she had ever known. But she left no forwarding address, or if she did the Carters never told me.

I was heartbroken and cried that night.

I never saw Jean again. I only hope she went on to meet someone who treated her well and gave her a good life.

During these years from age 16 to 19, I had clearly turned my back on God. I was doing things that were against God's laws, like bashing up homosexuals at the Cross and having lots of sex with girls. I was paying God back for abandoning me whilst at Charlton Boys' Home.

When I had overtime I earned good money, especially for my age. So for Mum's birthday I spent over one week's wages of about £16 on a cameo brooch and earrings which I had been paying off. On her birthday I gave it to her gift-wrapped. My mother said it was cheap-looking. With her accompanying me, she had me take it back to Stern's jewellery store in Newtown, where she wanted to exchange it for a much dearer Cameo set that cost over two week's wages. Reluctantly I arranged to pay the extra week's wages to satisfy her. I have never forgotten this incident: it always comes to mind on her birthday, 29 January.

My motorbike that I used in the main for transport to and from work always annoyed Mum immensely, maybe because of the noise of starting up in the morning while she was still asleep. Mum continued to nag me every day about my bike. One day in her temper she badly damaged the motor by hitting it with an axe. I had just come home from seeing my friends Davey and Ivan and with great shock the first thing I saw was the axe stuck in the bike, where she had left it no doubt for more dramatic appearance.

I was in deep shock that Mum would damage something I had worked so hard to buy. I went off my head and called her terrible names, but no swear words: I never swore at her or in front of her, ever. Vic, her de facto of by now about seven years, came to her rescue and threw a punch or two at me. He landed one punch on my face, which made me even more furious and I immediately laid into him, hitting him as hard as I could and at the same time pushing him out into the backyard. This gave me more room to avoid Mum trying to hit me from behind with a piece of timber. As well as fighting Vic, I had to keep an eye on her.

It did not take long and soon I had Vic laid out on the ground in submission. He was a mess, with blood pouring from his nose. Mum was calling me everything from her book of low-life expletives. I walked past her and walked to work, spending many hours waiting for my shift to start. She rang work to find out if I was coming home, because she knew it was payday and wanted the money for board on time. I was given an extra shift's overtime and did not finish work until seven Saturday morning.

I went home and she was waiting for her £10. I gave it to her and ignored her and Vic for a week or more.

When the shops opened I went up Botany Road to the pet shop where I bought horse meat for my dogs. It was mixed with a little kangaroo meat and sliced like steak. My dogs loved it fresh. I would buy about 20 pounds in weight of meat and break it up into seven-day packs, put six in the freezer and leave a few slices for that day in the fridge on a plate.

I went out that Saturday night and did not return until Sunday morning. First thing I did was go to the fridge to get the sliced pet meat to feed the dogs. I could not find it in the fridge, so I asked Mum if she had already fed the dogs and she said no. Then all hell broke loose as Mum and Vic realised they had eaten the horse meat by mistake.

I could not help myself: I went outside and laughed and laughed and thought: Well, I thought, this is God acting in His mysterious way to punish both of you for destroying my motorbike. Mum started her dramatic act, saying she was going to be sick. She blamed Vic for cooking the wrong meat. I said to them that they should see a doctor because horse and kangaroo meat is well known to give humans worms or worse still rabies, which has killed many people. Mum and Vic were not amused.

This episode still brings a smile to my face.

14

Army, girls and moving out at last

Prime Minister Robert Menzies had introduced National Service in 1951, and I had to register for National Service on my 18th birthday. I received a letter from the National Service Authority directing me to report for a "medical" at Mascot. On the appointed time and day I turned up for my medical check-up.

A few months later I received correspondence directing me to report to begin my three months initial training. I was a little apprehensive not knowing what to expect. After we had assembled, our names were called out and I was directed to waiting transport for my trip to Ingleburn Army Camp.

Our compulsory National Service Training consisted of 100 days straight of basic training, then the Citizens Military Forces for a further two years which included two full weeks training at Singleton each year plus monthly weekend camps and gatherings at Victoria Barracks. After the two years CMF we were all

Reserves until our four years were completed. During the last year we were not required for further training.

I loved my National Service. It brought out the best in me and allowed me to follow my boxing interests. But the strict military discipline did take time to get used to. I met many new friends and the army gave me a chance to express myself but most importantly National Service gave me a sense of responsibility. It also helped me wake up to myself about hating people.

When I boxed in the Brigade championships, I was thinking about hurting gays that were pictured in my mind as we boxed. One day I hit this chap really hard and I heard his head hit the canvas. I think in that instant it brought me back to my senses. I recall kneeling down next to him and lifting his head and praying he would be OK. The referee was yelling at me to get to my corner, but as others came into the ring to give support I stayed kneeled down. This was one of a few occasions when I hated myself. How happy and relieved I was when my opponent opened his eyes and tried to sit up. My silent prayer had been answered.

After that day I did not approach my fights with the same brutality. Looking back, I think this when I became a man and a better person. I realised that I no longer wanted to hurt or kill other people, including the homosexuals at the Cross.

There was a Sergeant Jones with whom I had had a fight one day whilst out on exercise. When I was beaten in the Brigade final, he was the first to congratulate me on a courageous fight. Sgt Jones and I had a good talk and at my request he arranged for my transfer after basic training to the Field Ambulance Corps. I had decided I just didn't have it in me to kill people, even in war. Little did I realise at that time that if I had been called up for war I had just placed myself in a more dangerous personal situation.

During my initial Army training, I came home a few times because I knew Mum never walked the dogs. One evening while still in uniform and walking my dog Snow along Erskineville Road near the Holy Trinity Church corner, I ran into a lovely girl I had seen a few times with my mates. She was a quiet girl and I had wanted to ask her out to a movie or something else. But I was reluctant because I hardly knew her, although I knew her sister Diana very well.

We began talking and she asked me about my dog. She was well dressed and you could see she was someone who cared about herself. She had this beautiful reddish long hair. I was attracted to her immediately. But next thing she was gone and I was dirty on myself for not asking her out. I continued to walk the dog but I could not get her out of my mind.

That unassuming, beautiful girl was Beryl Louisa MacFarlane, who in a few years' time would become my loving wife.

My initial 100 days of Army training were completed and I returned home to Erskineville to work at Crago's Flour Mill. Sadly the company was in decline with all the Colombo Plan orders completed, and they began putting men off. They cut down from three shifts to two. Soon my mates and I were given notice to leave.

I was only out of work a few days when I applied to the Koala Shirt Company for a dispatch and packing position advertised in *The Sydney Morning Herald*. Over 30 others applied for the position. I met a Mr Bush who said he would advise me if I had the job by telegram. I had applied for other jobs and already received a number of job offers. But that afternoon I received a telegram asking me to start at the Koala Shirt Company in Clarence Street, Sydney, in a building next to the Police Station.

Working at Koala Shirts was full-on, but I enjoyed the place and the other men I worked with.

It was about this time that Mum started to complain again about my dogs. Every day when I arrived home from work it was nag nag nag. Eventually her nagging over nothing was too much, so I advertised my Samoyeds in the *Herald* as a free giveaway. It did not take long for people to turn up on the Saturday morning and they promised a good home for Lady and Ruffy.

My heart was heavy and I was so sad to see them leave in cars, with me hoping I had done the right thing by them. I knew that I would never see them again. Mum did not appear to care: once again she had got her way.

After Lady and Ruffy were driven away, I went back inside the house. Mum pretended she was sad the dogs were gone. What an imposter, I thought to myself.

From this moment on I was determined to leave my mother's house. I decided to see if Warwick Cotten, a mate I had met through my National Service, had room at his house for a boarder. Subsequently Warwick's parents agreed to give me a room. As soon as I moved into the Cotten house at 14 Napoleon Road, Greenacre, I just knew life was going to be a lot better. I now had regular good meals and a nice warm bed and everything was so clean. Warwick's sister Sue was a good kid and I often joked around with her: she had a great sense of humour.

Each Wednesday night Wok (as we called Warwick) and I would drive in his Holden car, which was cream and light green, to Sylvania. Here I was introduced to playing tennis and I loved it. Occasionally we played on a Saturday morning at Haberfield with Wok's workmates.

Warwick and I also played rugby league during winter with Bankstown United, whose home ground was Bankstown Oval. On a Sunday night Wok and I used to go to the Irish National Club Dance at Surry Hills in Devonshire Street, not far from Central.

During our times at the Dance we met many nice girls and later a couple of good Catholic girls who were full of life. We started to take them out on a regular basis: Warwick took up

Come home, you little bastards

with Janette and I began taking out her sister Annie. They lived in a nice old full brick house. Their parents were real nice people with strong Catholic beliefs, as were the girls and their brother. Soon they were going with us to all our tennis nights.

I grew very fond of Annie. She was a virgin and said she was going to stay that way until she married. If she felt she ever sinned she would go to confession as fast as you can say Jack Robinson. I respected Annie for her discipline and her beliefs. But for a young man like myself, it was very difficult to be kissing a girl with much passion without going further.

One Friday I met her at her local station and I went into the cake shop and bought two meat pies, one each. "What are you doing Carl, buying meat pies on a Friday?" she asked. I did not understand the question until she explained that Catholics never eat meat on Fridays. She must have thought I was a heathen. I told her that as a Protestant the only day we never ate meat was Good Friday. So her religion was a true learning experience, which after the meat pie episode I fully respected and never offended her again.

I recall it was quite hot that summer and all of us spent a lot of time at Bondi or Coogee beaches. At the time I thought Warwick was in love with Janette, but he often turned up with other girls from work. Sometimes he would rush home from being with one girl to take another out. He could never be faithful to one girl.

One night I took Annie to a party which went very late. We had a great time: she was always full of laughter and enjoyed life to the full. We got a taxi to her home and as usual we sat on the verandah and kissed and cuddled and eventually I started to go beyond the boundaries. Soon I was full of lust and attempted to undress her, which at first she didn't object to. But after a while Annie burst out crying.

I asked her what was wrong. She explained how she felt sex

before marriage was wrong and being a virgin was how she wanted to remain. I was angry with myself and I told Annie I understood and not to worry because I would not go there again.

Annie told me she had never felt in love with a boy before and how she loved me so much. I knew she loved me: you can tell by the way a girl kisses you and by the length of time she would kiss and cuddle. Sometimes a kiss is more than a kiss. A kiss can tell you a lot about a person: there is no doubt about that.

Annie said that by going too far she would have to confess her sins that very next day. We talked on for a fair while. When I kissed her goodnight I was still embarrassed by my earlier behaviour.

I could not get Annie out of my mind, but I was too embarrassed to phone her. She phoned Mrs Cotten's place where I lived a number of times, but I never returned the calls. The last time I saw her was at our usual tennis night at Sylvania with her sister Janette, who Warwick was still taking out now and then. We spoke normally and never brought up that disastrous night when I had her in tears, but as time went by we stopped socialising together.

15

Meeting Beryl again

Some time later I bumped into Beryl MacFarlane again in the street. We got talking and I invited her out. I was 19 at the time and Beryl was 18.

One Friday night, I had arranged to take Beryl out and to meet her at 7pm outside Beberfalds retail store, which was on the corner opposite Sydney Town Hall. I arrived well before the scheduled time and waited. Time went by but there was no sign of her, and as 9.30 came and went I decided that she was not coming. Upset and feeling rejected, I went back to Erskineville.

It turned out Beryl had also arranged to meet up with her boyfriend Tony Bull that night. She had been going through a traumatic time with Tony, who it appears was always putting her down. She later told me he often called her Plain Jane and compared her to other girls, which hurt Beryl a great deal.

When I started taking Beryl out I had that feeling she still cared for Tony, even though he had hurt her badly. But I persisted, because I loved her and loved being in her company. She did not say much and never expected very much from a boyfriend. Beryl did not expect you to spend heaps of money on her. I tried to see her as often as I could.

One day Beryl told me she was moving to Greenacre to live with her sister Fay Newton, which came as a surprise. But I thought at least she would be with family and would no longer have her father telling her not to come around to his house during meal times because they could not afford it, as he once did.

Each evening after work I would catch a train to Lakemba from Town Hall Station to meet up with Beryl. Then we would catch the local bus together to Greenacre.

One night on the bus Beryl told me she would not be seeing me again. I was shocked and lost for words: I assumed she still cared for Tony Bull. I left Beryl at the Macquarie and Roberts Road corner and slowly walked home, asking myself why.

It must have been obvious I was upset, because when I got home Warwick asked me: "What's wrong Carl? You don't seem yourself." After we had all finished the evening meal, I just sat in the lounge room and watched television for a while. They all noticed how quiet I was. I went to bed early after saying goodnight to everyone.

I got no sleep that night. I just lay in bed wide awake thinking only of Beryl. I was really upset and lay there crying. The more I thought of Beryl, the worse I became. I didn't know if she realised how much she had hurt me.

One night her brother-in-law Dennis Newton came knocking on the Cottens' front door and told me Beryl wanted to see me. So a little later I went up to see what she wanted. Beryl told me she had no money to pay her board and was visibly upset. If I recall correctly, Beryl had lost her job as a waitress up near Oxford Street, Sydney. Even though she had hurt me like I had never been hurt before, I still cared for her. I offered her the money and did my best to help her. Later we went for a drive and she started talking about how she was not sure if she still loved Tony. We talked a lot and finally she said she realised it was really me she wanted. Eventually we parked and stopped the car and talked, then kissed and made love for hours into the early morning. We then drove to Beryl's sister's house and I went home.

Fay and Dennis Newton, who Beryl lived with, always made me feel very welcome. Beryl and I would just sit and watch television or go for a drive. Of a night Dennis and Fay would leave us alone and we would kiss and cuddle and make love until the early hours of the morning and then I would go home. I would grab a few hours sleep and wake up worn out. Every spare moment I had I would spend with Beryl.

A year or so after I had bumped into Beryl again and asked her out, we decided we should get a flat of our own and live together. I was about 21 and Beryl was 20. We got engaged and were deeply in love. I adored her so much and knew I wanted to spend my whole life with her. I still adore her.

Beryl and I were married at St Stephen's Church in Newtown. Warwick Cotten was my best man and Beryl's sister Diane her matron of honour. Diane's husband Manuel would not step inside the church because he was Roman Catholic and ours was a Church of England marriage. I remember thinking: what harm could it do if Manuel sat inside a different denomination church? He wasn't even a practising Catholic.

We had around 30 family and friends at the marriage ceremony. Mum came but Dad did not: he said he did 'not want to be in the same room as that vile woman', meaning my mother.

Poor Beryl was very ill on our wedding day: I do not know how she got through the day and the dinner afterwards. She was in the early stages of morning sickness, but she still looked beautiful in her little hat and a nice green dress with puff-like sleeves that her sister Fay had made especially for our wedding. All our family and friends shared our happiness.

A photographer was hired to take the wedding photographs, but sadly we could not afford to buy them at that time. A few years later we tried to get them, but it was too late: they had been destroyed. So we have no images of our special day.

Without doubt this day, 23 January, 1960, was the happiest day of both of our lives. For the first time in my life, I knew what true love was all about.

Beryl came from a very poor family, made much worse by her dad Harry always trying to find a way out of poverty by betting with the SP bookmakers and looking for a big win. Beryl loved her father deeply, but like many men from his time he could not reciprocate or show a loving side. Beryl's mother Maisie suffered from chronic anxiety and depression. But at least Harry and Maisie did not drink, so Beryl never had to put up with drunken parties.

Beryl gave me the inspiration to work hard with two full-time jobs to achieve our first goal, and that was to buy and own our first home and provide a loving and safe place to bring up children. We were determined to make better lives for our kids than we had had, and to make sure they never went without anything.

16

New beginnings

It was after our first child Linda had been born and during Beryl's pregnancy with our second child John that we had saved enough money to buy our own home in Smithfield. We had chosen all the colours and the roof tiles and the outside was painted white with blue trimmings. The block was a quarter acre with no sewer connected: we had to do with a dry pan, which was picked up once a week by the council men. We had very little furniture and very little of anything else, but we were happy to have a new home for the four of us. To us, our small three-bedroom fibro house was heaven. It was something we had dreamed about for a long time; at last it was a reality.

Mum was not too bad at this time. On occasions she would visit us, but mostly we called in to see her. I think she tried to behave herself in front of Beryl.

But I knew from experience that Mum's good behaviour would not last. There were a couple of horrible incidents, but by far the worst one occurred a couple of years later when our kids were growing up. We had been invited to Mum's for a meal, but when we arrived the house was one big mess. There we were, me, Beryl, Linda, John and Kathleen, our youngest. No sooner had we walked into what looked like a rubbish dump than my mother told us that Vic had said we had had to get married because Beryl was pregnant. This was a complete fabrication: they both knew we had planned our marriage before we even knew Beryl was pregnant.

Beryl was very upset by Mum's stupid comment. But Mum and Vic carried on making caustic remarks, mainly at each other. Then Vic retired to the bedroom, closely followed by Mum. She began screaming out loud that Vic was hitting her. Vic was not hitting her at all: it was all for effect, hoping I would come in and have a go at Vic. But I did not take the bait.

Mum then did a terrible thing in front of the children. She came running up the hall with a large carving knife raised in front of her, charging at us. I knew that she had lost her marbles and quick as I could I pushed Beryl and our children out the front door, desperately telling them to make a fast retreat. Then I too retreated like greased lightning. We did not have time to get to our car, so we all ran up Rochford Street with her chasing us with the knife, calling out obscenities like only Mum could. I don't mind staying I was a little scared, so I can imagine how my family must have felt.

Soon after she stopped chasing us and returned to her asylum. We stayed up on Erskineville Road for ages, then in the darkness I crept silently back to our car, started the engine real fast and quietly drove up the street where I picked up my family.

If you ask Beryl or any of our children about that day, they will still tell you how scared they were. None of us spoke to her again for many years after that terrible night. Mum never apologised to us.

Mum's de facto partner Vic, despite everything, loved Mum very much. This became very evident when Mum passed away on 25 November 1988, having died in her sleep from a heart attack. Vic rang to tell us the sad news. He was so distressed he struggled to get the words out. At the funeral Vic was so upset he could hardly speak to any of the family or to Mum's close friends. I had not wanted to go to Mum's funeral, but Beryl convinced me it was the right thing to do. I felt nothing at the time: it was not till some time later that the sadness started to seep in.

One week later, Vic phoned me and was emotionally out of control. He had been walking around the graveyard for a long time searching for Mum's grave. "Carlie," he asked, "Can you come out to Rookwood and help me find the grave?" I told him to wait near the closed Anglican office and I would be there as quick as possible. Arriving there 30 minutes later, I found Vic crying his heart out. I tried my best to comfort him and even though his crying was relentless, I was able to assist him to the car and I drove down a track opposite the Anglican office to where we were only 10 yards or so from Mum's grave.

Vic got out and said, "I've walked past this area over and over." We walked over to the grave and Vic fell on his knees, crying in uncontrolled pain. I knelt beside him for about an hour and I could feel his pain as his body shook all over. I had my arm around him and asked him if he wanted to go home. He said, "No, I'll stay here as I have nothing now to go home to." I stayed with him for another hour or so and then he asked me to go, as he wanted to be alone with Mum. As I drove off, he was still kneeling at the grave near the flowers he had brought with him.

Two years later Vic passed away, never getting over Mum's death. We suspect Vic had just lost the will to live. He was a decent man, but like all of us he was not perfect. I do know he did everything in his power to make Mum happy.

When our son John was six years old, I began taking him to soccer with Fairfield Heights Club at Prospect View Park. I soon became very actively involved in the soccer club and became secretary. I built the club's teams up from six to 54. Each year I doorknocked every home in the area and went to each school recruiting boys to play soccer for Fairfield Heights. We were the biggest junior club in Australia for many years.

In 1988, I was held up by two men at gunpoint at a petrol station where I was working. It was a really ugly and terrifying experience, with a gun held to my mouth while another was pointed at me. Following this incident Beryl was keen for us to move, so the following year we sold our Smithfield home and, after 26 years, moved to the new home we had built on some land we had bought at Tuross Head, overlooking the water.

I was only 53 when we moved to Tuross Head, but we decided we had just about enough to live on, so I took up just part-time work at the Moruya Golf Club and the Monarch Hotel. I also got very actively involved in the local community and in politics, becoming secretary of the local branch of the ALP and also for the State Electorate of Bega and the Federal Electorate of Eden-Monaro.

In 2003 we sold our beautiful seaside home and returned to Sydney, mainly because we were getting older and it was more convenient for us in case of sickness but also because we wanted to spend more time with our children and grandchildren. We bought a home at Ambarvale and we have been here ever since. This was a good move as far as our health was concerned, as both of us have subsequently suffered some major health problems.

17

Reflections

In 2004, I gave evidence about my time in Charlton to the Senate Affairs References Committee, which was writing a report on Australians who experienced institutional care as children. They subsequently published two reports: *Forgotten Australians* in August 2004 and *Protecting Vulnerable Children: A National Challenge* in March 2005.

The decision to give evidence to this hearing was a really hard one. I had never spoken to my wife Beryl or any of my family about what happened to me during my time at Charlton. Even after giving my evidence, I only told Beryl in bits over time. She was angry with me for not having told her earlier, because it was the first time I had kept something a secret from her. I also had to seek help to deal with my demons, which I did through Anglicare Professional Standards Unit. They have been wonderful. I have put more than 100 inmates in touch with them over the years.

Why did I decide to give evidence and drag all the bad memories out again? In some ways it's a lot easier just to suppress horrible experiences from the past. But once the opportunity to give evidence arose through the Senate Inquiry, I just felt I had to get involved in order to try to shed some light on what had happened to me and others, and try to bring some of the criminal paedophiles to justice. I did not want these mongrels to get away with what they had done.

Through this process and more recently the Royal Commission into Institutional Responses to Child Sex Abuse, I've got in contact with lots of other inmates from my days at Charlton. Just a few of their stories are in the Appendix. I have also been forced to think a lot about who I am and how I survived such a horrible upbringing. All that thinking and grappling with my past is what led to this book.

When I look back now on my childhood days, I often ask myself: why was I not born into a normal family? Why was my mother so selfish that she just considered Neville and me a nuisance and wanted us out of the way? And how did I get through all this, including what happened at Charlton, and get to lead a normal, happy adult life, while many other inmates were unable to? I think I can only try to answer this by looking back at both the bad and the good parts of my life.

Mum's continuous infidelity and selfishness hurt all of us. But despite her behaviour and how she treated us, as a child I still wanted my mother and her love more than anything on this earth. I believe Mum just couldn't give love: she could only accept love from others. As time went by, my unconditional love for Mum diminished to the point that I could not bring myself to kiss her or hug her. I had judged and condemned her, and could not find it within me to forgive her all her sins against us.

What about my father? Why did he not realise that walking out on us would have adverse consequences that could hurt us all our lives? I still feel that, despite my mother's appalling behaviour, Dad had no right walking out on Neville and me and leaving us in such an unhealthy environment. He left us boys in an unfriendly and unloved situation with Mum where we were often starving and cold. He should have given more consideration to our needs and fought for us more to ensure we had a healthy upbringing. Reg had a choice, but he walked away from his responsibility into the arms of a much younger woman to begin his new family. We were excluded. Yes, Dad had every right to leave Mum: that goes without saying. But he failed badly in my eyes, because he never considered what was best for Neville and me. We were incidental, born from Dad and Mum's love relationship and then suffering from their hatred of each other. The truth, Reg, is this: you failed Neville and me dismally. Reg died in 2015 in his 99th year.

I partly blame my Mum for this. I don't know what my father was like as a child, but I do know he came from a loving Christian family. Yet as a parent, like my Mum, he could not give love himself. I think my father was damaged for life by my mother and her horrible ways. Even with his second wife Beryl, who was a real family-orientated lady and ten years younger, he could not show true love. If he did not know where she was he was always suspicious, thinking she was out with other men. My mother gave him a life sentence of suspicion, jealousy and hate: for many years after my mother died in 1988, Reg Beauchamp still carried enormous hate towards her and referred to our mother as a vile and an unfaithful bastard of a woman, "no better than a whore". These were his bitter words.

I often wonder: did Dad ever really love my mother? How can you love someone and next instant hate someone you profess to love? And how can a man carry such hate all his life without becoming a bitter person? I no longer feel hatred towards my mother, the way my father did right up to the day he died. Maybe seeing what it did to Dad helped me realise how destructive hatred can be. Maybe my later research into Mum's upbringing also helped. I discovered that her mother and father were related and so they could never marry. A fictitious name was put on the birth certificates of my Mum and her siblings. While I know Mum's mother, Ma Kate, loved her, Mum was a real rebel as a child. I don't know if this and the way she turned out was in part because she knew about her parents, but maybe it was.

On a Pacific cruise on the Fair Princess about 15 years ago, I told my father I loved him as I gave him a hug, asking him why he had never been there for me. His response was to pull away without saying a single word. Beryl apologised later, saying: "That's how he's always been."

My father once told me that he was never aware that we spent years in Church homes. I'll never know if that was true.

What about the paedophiles at Charlton? When I left Charlton in 1953 to go home, I also left behind my faith in God. I often wondered why God allowed these dirty paedophiles to hurt me and so many other inmates over and over again. How was I ever going to forget the constant pain and crying in the dormitory of all those young boys?

In the course of organising a reunion of Charlton inmates in 2010, getting involved in trying to encourage inmates to seek support and counselling and then putting evidence together for the Royal Commission into Child Sex Abuse, I got in contact with many of my former inmates. I learnt just how much stress and depression stayed with many of them throughout their lives. A lot of them blame Sachisthal for what has been for them a life of misery and never-ending suffering, with depression, so many broken relationships and a number of suicides.

How could so many so-called Christians, whose job was to look after very young and vulnerable children, do the things they did? I used to think Sachisthal was in some ways a well-meaning man, a bit brutal and naïve in the way he trusted the people around him but basically not a bad person. At the time many of the boys, including myself, just thought all the sexual inspections he made were the normal thing everywhere. But from talking to other inmates, I have learnt that I was very naïve. Indeed in some ways Sachisthal was even more guilty than the other paedophiles: he was in charge, and it was he who allocated out boys to his paedophile mates. I now think Sachisthal was a sick and very disturbed man.

But I do not hate him. That may sound surprising given that one of the things I am currently doing is trying to ensure that his OBE is withdrawn. But I know in my heart that this is not motivated by hatred but by a desire for justice, just as my decision in 2004 to drag out all the old memories I had been suppressing and give evidence to the Senate Committee was motivated by a desire for justice. We weren't brave enough when we were young to call out and try to bring these paedophiles to justice. But if we don't do it now, how do we know this sort of thing won't just continue over and over?

What about the good people who helped me get over my upbringing and become, I hope, a reasonable bloke, husband and father? I do not know how other men think and feel about that special woman in their lives. But I do know that no man could ever love a woman as I loved Beryl, then and now. Beryl is the main reason I got my life and happiness back, and why I have enjoyed life ever since. If I had to, I would gladly forfeit my life if it meant saving hers.

Beryl has also been a wonderful mother to our children. In our early days, I saw her go without so much so that our children could have something better than what she and I had had. I pray that all our children will over time fully comprehend how fortunate they have been having Beryl as their mother.

My grandmother, Ma Kate, was also a great source of love for me, even during the worst periods with Mum. She taught me about manners and respect. She taught me to always say please and thank you, to treat women with respect, and that a real man never hits a woman and men should always walk on the footpath nearest the road and women walk on the inside. This was to be protective, she always said. She taught me to address adults always with Mr or Mrs and she taught me so much of what was right and what was wrong. When she lived with us for a short period after my father left she taught me to say grace for the meals she had prepared. I was taught to open and close doors for women and to pull out a chair for them to sit.

I have also never forgotten the love and understanding that was shown to me as a very sad and disturbed little boy at Carlingford Boys' Home. Matron Hill's kindness has never been forgotten. She truly cared. I've often thought of her and included her in many a prayer, asking God to bless her.

I think that being at Carlingford Boys' Home gave me a better understanding of what life could be and should be about. Two things they taught me stand out: love and understanding; and to have faith in Jesus that everything would turn out for the best.

There was not much love at Charlton, but there was one exception: Chaplain Ray Weir, to whom I dedicate this book. From the first time I saw him in Yasmar Court in 1950 when I was just 13, I could see that the chaplain was a profoundly compassionate and practical man of God. On first meeting him, I could feel the warmth of his love.

All of us boys at Charlton loved Chaplain Weir. He always told us: "I am here with you always." At the time I used to think he meant he would always be with us, but now I realise he was talking about God. He never let us down. The first thing he would do on his visits to Charlton was to search out all the boys he knew and ask how we were. Everyone was enchanted by his beautiful smile. No matter how down you were and emotionally upset, his smile and warmth would lift you from the paralysing depression or anger you might have been feeling. And like a miracle you were happy again, even if it were only for a short period while he was with you.

Chaplain Weir was our friend. We trusted him, but still none of us could shame ourselves by speaking about the horrible paedophiles within and outside of the boys' home.

I came very close to telling him what was going on at Charlton once. But I couldn't quite do it, partly because I somehow felt that if I told him it would reflect badly on me rather than the perpetrators, and partly because I knew Sachisthal would deny the accusations, even if they came from Jesus Christ himself.

I recall after I'd been an inmate at Charlton for about one year Chaplain Weir came to our monthly Sunday Fellowship Tea. I was very sad this day because I had not seen my mother for four months, and even though I knew she did not care I could not stop the oceans of tears flowing down my face as Ray Weir stopped to talk to me. He placed his hand on my face ever so gently and asked me what the problem was. I told him and he assured me he would contact her and in front of all the other boys said a prayer asking God to help me in my moment of sadness. I still remember imagining at that moment, as a little boy, that God and Ray Weir were as one.

After I left the Home I never saw the Reverend Ray Weir again. He died in 1978, only 55 years old. A few years back, I started doing a lot of research on him in order to put forward a case to have him awarded an MBE. But I discovered, after having spoken to a lot of his family, friends and acquaintances and putting together a lot of material, that you cannot be awarded an MBE posthumously.

There is an old Jewish saying: "Whoever saves a single life saves an entire universe." If you think about this saying you begin to understand its meaning, and if you understand this, then you immediately realise the Reverend Ray Weir was truly a remarkable man, living the true Christian life to help people like myself. As I write this I can see Ray Weir's smiling face as clearly as it was back in the early 1950s.

As I look back on the darkest periods of my early life, I realise that, while my mother never loved us, there were enough people around me who did show me love and compassion that I never lost sight of what love was and what it could achieve. I've already spoken about the love from Ma Kate, from Matron Hill in Carlingford, from Chaplain Weir when I was in Charlton. But I also remember the love and compassion from people like Mr and Mrs Blacket at Harbord; like Mr Laws in my Opportunity Class at Erskineville Primary School; and the parents of some of my Erskineville friends who knew how hard life was for Neville and me and often found a spare hot meal for us on Sundays.

I think because of all these good people in my life I never fully gave up hope. So when the love of my life, Beryl, came on the scene, I knew I had to grab the opportunity and create a new loving environment for us both and for our kids. That's a big part of how I got through.

What influence have my brothers and half-brothers had on my life? To be honest, the only one I have stayed close to is Neville, who shared with me all the horror stories I have recounted about growing up with Mum. When Neville left home the day after Mum pretended to gas herself, I saw a lot of him for a while, but then he disappeared and we did not see him again for a decade.

Neville had gone bush, working at Coonabarabran, clearing scrub and later making his way to Bourke and Wanaaring where he worked on sheep and cattle stations. Later in life he moved to Tibooburra with his little baby girl: he had left Wanaaring after returning from a bush job to find his wife playing up with a local young man. His daughter Kathy was placed in a church boarding school at Tibooburra whilst he lived at Fortville

Gate near Cameron's Corner where he worked as a dingo fence ranger. He lived there until 1988 when he retired through back injuries and bought a home at Tuross Head where he lives today. His daughter Kathy lives near Canberra and she has three children.

After divorcing my mother, my father Reginald Beauchamp married Beryl Chudleigh and had two boys: Ken born in 1944 and Alan born 1946. Both had failed first marriages. Ken had few interests in life and died at Berry aged 53. He had alcoholic problems during his life. Alan lives with his second wife at Albion Park. Like his father, Alan is a rather quiet person with very little interest in sport or current affairs. Alan had two sons, Keith and Wayne, both of whom were very good rugby league players, with Keith playing first grade for the St George Dragons for many years.

My other half-brother, Ian, Victor and Mum's child, received a much better life than Neville and me but like us he had to put up with the drunken parties and the fighting between Vic and my mother. When the opportunity came he took up a career in nursing and went to Africa for a few years. On returning he married and he and his wife bought a house on the Queensland coast and a franchise with LJ Hooker. Later they moved to Tasmania where they operate an LJ Hooker franchise. They never had children.

Some years ago I had decided that I could not leave this earth without first placing a memorial over my mother's and her father's graves at Rookwood and of course also my grandmother Kate's, who is buried in the Old Catholic section. Believing that Adrian and Neville would want to be involved with the wording and cost I contacted them. Neville said he did not have the money to contribute and offered to pay a share later on. I told Neville to forget it and I would pay his share.

What of my own children? Linda, our firstborn, was one of the first children to attend the new Smithfield West Public School. She was one of the quiet children in her year but did well. However, she had many difficult moments dealing with bullies, I think because she was quiet and never outspoken. She married Larry Clarke who was in the Army. They live near Maitland, where Larry is a security officer, and have two children, Tammy and Steven. Linda has not been in good health.

Our second child John was very good at soccer from a young age. He progressed to a stage where talent scouts from district clubs were interested in him, but John declined their offers, wishing to stay with his friends. John married Rhonda Dodds and they had four girls. They moved to Tuross Heads far too young and found it difficult paying off their home, as work was hard to come by. As the years passed, John's marriage came under pressure and he got divorced. John later married for the second time to Lisa, and they had one boy named Riley. John works for IGA at Moruya. Lisa died in 2015 after a lengthy fight against cancer. She was only 51.

Our third child Kathleen was born in 1964. Kathleen has always been outgoing and found mixing with others very easy. From an early age she excelled at all sports, particularly athletics and swimming. But after her first year at high school she showed no more interest in sport, which was sad because she had so much natural talent she could have gone right to the top.

Kathleen has two children, Katelyn and Kruse, with her partner Lowry Ngati. They live near us, and Kate calls in each day to see if we need any help. She has been a wonderful daughter in every way possible.

Our youngest son Paul epitomises what has made Australia strong: hard work. As a young boy growing up, Paul would make a bit of extra money by going door to door asking for work mowing lawns or washing cars or gardening, and saving what he earned above his weekly pocket money. By the time he was 16 he had saved enough to buy my two-year-old Skyline car from me. Paul held a variety of jobs in Sydney before moving to Moruya just after he married, where he and his wife Brenda bought their first home. Since then Paul has been self-employed with a number of successful business ventures. Paul and Brenda have three girls.

Even with such a horrible childhood I would rather not change the past. Changing the bad bits would risk also changing some of the good things, and probably change who I am in the process. I am happy with nearly all of the choices I have made throughout my life and the love that it eventually brought me. Most of all the hard, difficult childhood days gave me the motivation to make life for my family better than mine and to be a big part in the lives of my children, grandchildren and great grandchildren.

I hope I have been a good father. Of course there are always things that you could have done better. Certainly none of our children have brought us great worries, which is a statement that not all families can claim. Taking everything into consideration, Beryl and I have been truly blessed. We hope that the standards we have set in place will also be applied by our grandchildren and our great grandchildren.

My reward from my horrible experiences when I was young is that it taught me to be a forgiving man and to love all my family deeply, especially my dear wife Beryl. But an equally great reward is that I have learnt not to hate anybody. Forgiving is one of the most important things in life, because it takes away all hatred that the mind will otherwise harbour.

I end my story here. I have been truthful in everything I have recounted. Some things I'm not proud of, but as I said, I wouldn't want to change very much. Overall I've had a very fortunate life.

Experiences of other Charlton inmates

In 2010, some of us who were inmates at Charlton together held a reunion. It took me three years to organise this event because it was very hard tracking people down. I did this mainly through a series of advertisements in newspapers and then also by word of mouth.

In the course of organising the event and trying to organise a subsequent reunion, I talked to inmates about their time in Charlton. Many of them had not spoken to their family or anyone else about what had happened to them at Charlton, but the old suppressed memories started flooding back. Some former inmates did not want to talk to me at all about their experiences or even come to the reunion, which is not surprising given what they had been through.

Below are just a few of the stories that were told to me. Some of the inmates I contacted got back to me by letter or email, and others spoke to me by phone. Where they wrote to me I have quoted their words directly. Some of them were happy to be named and others less so, so I have just used first names for all of them.

Experiences of other Charlton inmates

MERVYN, AT CHARLTON 1956-1957

I was the youngest of nine children, I was taken away from my mother when I was only three years of age with two of my elder sisters. I was ripped out of my mother's arms at the rail station and taken to Brisbane by Welfare Queensland. Then I went to a foster home on a farm at Caboolture. I was treated OK, in one way but not that good. It broke my mother's heart, which eventually killed her, I only saw her twice after being taken away. The last time was when I was 15, just before she died. My father was gone in 1942: he died after he came back from World War II. I did not meet most of my brothers and sisters until I was a lot older. Then an older sister got custody of me when I was 13 years old. She took me to Sydney with her Muslim husband.

I was put to work in their fish shop at Randwick. There was no pay, he was very hard on me, and in the end we came to fighting. So I left and slept in the streets for a few days. I then went to the Welfare in the City and the person there said they have a place for me to go. They did not tell me it was a Boys' Home. I was put into the dormitory for a while and given regular cold showers early each morning. I worked in the kitchen. I was then sent out to work assembling lawn mowers. I received no wages. I was then shifted over to the adjacent building [Strathmore] into one of the top attic rooms. There were bed bugs and all. I was never given medical or dental treatment.

The first night there I was dragged out of bed in the middle of the night and raped by name I have forgotten, he also use to bully me in the yard with his mates. Also at showers George from the Home used to try and penetrate me, so Carl it was not a happy time for me, this messed up my whole life. At 21 years of age I tried to suicide in Brisbane. I hope you can read my terrible writing and thank you ever so much for what you did for me,

I was lucky I saw your advert in the *Daily Telegraph*, as it was a neighbour's paper I had a loan of. I could fill 20 pages if I told you everything, Thank you once again.

ALAN 1952–?

I arrived at Charlton Church of England Boys' Home in 1952. My first sight of the dull, uncared for property was one of profound pain considering the hyperbole from the magistrate at Albion Street Children's Court. He said, the home was of great beauty with surrounding gardens and with loving staff that were second to none. But in reality, there were no nice buildings or beautiful gardens and the staff were far from loving.

I was going on 14 and charged with being uncontrollable, this was not true, I had been thrown out of home by my drunken father, I had nowhere to go and for months I lived on the streets and slept in parks around Newtown. My favourite place to sleep was in the cemetery behind the Newtown church. Here I stashed my few belongings, hidden under a flat gravestone. The stash consisted of one blanket and a few warm clothes that I got for nothing from the St Vincent's second hand shop. To get enough food to live on I went through the garbage of the bread bakery and the nearby fish shop. When desperate I pinched people's milk money left out each night on their doorstep.

I hated Charlton, especially the German superintendent [Sachisthal], he hated me and often gave me a bashing, once the kraut broke my arm, when he bashed me with a square long piece of wood. The bone was sticking out and I was in pain, I asked for medical help, but nobody listened to me. Two days later an officer, Mr Norman, drove me to hospital at Newtown. When my arm was better I thought about skipping away, then one night the Nazi woke us up in the middle of the night and he marched us to the shower room, made us undress in the cold yard, there was about 20 of us, he made us all have cold showers, then without drying ourselves he lined us outside in the cold for an hour whilst he examined our private parts, he made fun of our small parts and gave us a lecture on masturbation. Then when finished he told us to get back to bed. The next day, during school hours, I did a skip.

For weeks I lived around Circular Quay, living from garbage tins and to break the day up I went back and forth to Manly. One day whilst getting off a tram along King Street Newtown I fell on to the road. When I got up, there was a policeman and he grabbed me and took me to gaol. I finished up in the boys' gaol at Gosford until I was 18 years old. I joined the army and later married and we had five children. Sometimes I think about those bad days and thank my lucky stars I did not finish up a criminal and spending time incarcerated or worse still a drunk or on drugs. My life has been one of many rewards from hard work. I live on the Central Coast and my garden is my life.

JOHN 1954-1960

I write this to put on record but please keep my address to yourself Carl as I have no intention whatsoever of telling my family about my horrible childhood, just respect my wishes is all I ask of you. I was brought to Charlton by the police, I had been brought to the Glebe home from the Yasmar Children's Court. My father had deserted my brothers and me and our mum could not cope, she became very ill and was taken to hospital and that was the last time I ever saw her. I was around nine years old and was being looked after by our grandmother out at Herne Bay and we lived in old army huts. It was about 1952 and I refused to go to school because I had no decent clothing and no shoes. By the time I was about 10 years the Child Welfare arrested me and took me away.

Experiences of other Charlton inmates

About early 1954 I was placed at Charlton Boys' Home at Glebe and classed as uncontrollable. The spiked haired Mr Sachisthal took me in and he gave me some new and old clothing and shoes and showed me to the big dormitory and showed me my bed and locker. I recall throwing the clothing on the bed, next instant he punched me in the head and I fell to the floor and he kicked me in the head.

He told me he would not tolerate insolence and to get down to the shower room and wash the blood off my face, I asked him where was the showers? He replied "what" what about addressing me as Sir you little bastard, and without warning he punched the hell out of me, then marched me to the showers. He watched me undress and shower, perving on my body. He told me to go dress in the yard clothing and report to his office.

I walked into his office and he screamed at me telling me I had not knocked first, then he told me all the rules and expected me to work hard to earn my keep, because I was just a bludger with nobody contributing to my keep. He warned me to shut up and only talk when he asked me anything. My head was still profusely bleeding from a deep cut above my left eye. He then looked at it and took me in the truck to hospital at Newtown where they put in a dozen stiches. He told me to tell the doctor "that I fell down the steps".

One day coming home from church, I went into a shop and bought lollies with the money I kept and did not put into the church offering plate. By the time I left the shop all the Home boys were way out of sight. I ate my lollies and as I entered the lane, I could see near the gate Mr Sachisthal waiting for me, he called me a thief and punched me in the face and he loosened two teeth and I had a bleeding nose.

He took me over to the old building that was being renovated and locked me in a small room. He left me there all night and on Monday morning he let me out. He told me to shower and get ready for school, this I did and lined up and marched to school. I had not eaten since breakfast Sunday morning and boy was I hungry. At lunch time all the home boys went to the usual place to pick up our jam sandwiches, the boy in charge handed them out to everyone except me, he had explicit orders that I was to have nothing. After school I arrived back to the home, got dressed in the yard clothes and Sachisthal ordered me to get a glass of water and marched me to the small room and locked me in. On Tuesday morning he opened the door at dawn, had me do my chores and told me I could have breakfast.

I was starving and I ate the porridge plate clean, never in my life had such terrible porridge tasted so good. Well after this punishment I never bought lollies again with the church money. Everything got better and he stopped picking on me as much. Then as a reward for being good he allowed me out one weekend with one of his friends, a Mr Menzies, he took me and another boy to his house near Bulli.

This turned out to be a real nightmare and my mate and I were sexually abused for two days by these two friends of Mr Sachisthal. I was glad when the Sunday afternoon arrived, when we were driven back to the home and dropped off. On arrival, Mr Sachisthal was waiting, I told him what his friends had done to us and that I still was bleeding from my backside. He said I was a liar, he then sent for the other boy who denied anything untoward had occurred. He threatened to send me to Mt Penang. Sachisthal took me to the shower and watched and then he ordered me to bend over so as he could inspect my backside. He was very rough, he told me to wake up to myself and to stop lying, and he concluded that I had piles. He marched me to the old building and locked me in the small room.

After this he treated me very bad and gave me the worst jobs and every time he saw me he would bash me across the head and call me a trouble maker. He had me on full-time kitchen duty and this was I had to prepare all the vegetables every day and permanently be on scullery duty.

During this time I had to serve the meals to Sachisthal and staff, I would be told by Miss Craig which meal was for each of the staff. When no one was looking I always brought up heaps of golly and spit it onto Sachisthal's meal and I would pick my nose and rub snot into his bread. One day I urinated into the staff teapot and placed it in front of Sachisthal and he poured out the tea and drank it. I laughed my head off as I heard him say, "I always like my cuppa tea" so after that every chance I got I would urinate in the staff teapot. A few times I near got caught, in fact I did get caught once by one of the Lawrence boys, lucky for me he was happy to be in on the joke and was also pleased I was getting back, as best I could.

The years after this went fast and I was always treated as the bad boy by Sachisthal. He never locked me up again but he could never resist punching me in the head and giving me the most terrible chores. One morning in his rage because I was late to a line up, he punched me in the stomach and for days I was in great pain. And as a further punishment he put me on kitchen duties and I purposely saved a little poo on a piece of paper and I rubbed poo on one side of his chops. Nothing was said, so I took it he enjoyed the extra garnish.

Well the sexual attacks happened a few more times and when I was 16 I left Charlton for good. I then, on my own, began a new life, a new beginning. My life has been very good. If I dwell on my Charlton days, I get very depressed, so I find being positive and my faith in Jesus helps me overcome what they did to me. So forgiveness is much better than holding hate inside me. Through hard work I have brought up a family, married for nearly 50 years. I believe that good can overcome bad, that is, if you give it a chance. I feel that my life has been a fortunate one, if I had held the hate in me after leaving Charlton I would have ended in gaol, but somehow fate has been kind to me, above everything else my faith in Jesus.

KEVIN 195?-?

I saw your advert in the *Telegraph* about a reunion; I can't recall any of the names you mentioned. I have had a sad life and I have suffered depression and I drink far too much and I have been divorced twice which has been my own fault. I have never been able to control my temper and I hate myself for the terrible bashings I have given both my wives and my children. I live a life alone now with constant nightmares reminding me of my horrible childhood at the Charlton Boys' Homes at Glebe and at Bowral and at Gosford a place for bad boys who were out of control.

I put a great deal of my torment down to being bashed at Charlton especially at Glebe where the bloke in charge with the crewcut hated me and he often forced me to eat porridge with grubs in it. When I spoke to you on the phone, you asked me if I had ever been sexually abused and did I need help from the church.

The answer is yes, I was raped by one of the officers, whose name I can't remember, he wore glasses, and I recall that because I broke them on purpose when he attacked me in the old building that was being repaired. As for help from the church, I can do without their help, where were they when I was bashed and raped at Glebe? If I change my mind I will contact you, but thanks again, I think you are a good man trying to help us old boys. But it is too late for me.

ALLAN 1956-1957

Allan was discarded by his mother as an infant, never knew his father and was cared for by his granny. At an infant age he was sent to Royleston State Boys Home, in Glebe Point Road, then later to Charlton Boys' Home aged seven.

Allan was an emotional little boy with many psychological problems, who had been dumped at Charlton by his mother who obviously did not want him.

Allan recalls crying every day. He recalls that one day he could not stand it any longer and with an Aboriginal boy, Dinky Davis, he ran away. Finding themselves lost in Sydney after getting the tram from Glebe, they just wandered around endlessly hoping to find someone who cared. The police requested information from the boys, then took them to Regent Street Police Station. Soon they were back at Charlton, where Allan says he was punished even more. Things went from bad to worse. He was assaulted physically and sexually, by two men in charge at the Home and by some older boys, with no one to turn to.

RON 1953-1963

Ron phoned me in response to my advert in the *Daily Telegraph* on 10 February 2011. We spoke in general about his ten years in Charlton, which he entered as a six-year-old unwanted child. Sachisthal had retired the year before Ron left, and Ray Menzies became Superintendent. Menzies often took Ron to his South Coast cottage near Coalcliff where Menzies sexually assaulted him many times over the years, as did other paedophiles including Bob Davies who also had a South Coast holiday cottage, and Cecil Boyton who also sexually assaulted boys in the ablutions block.

The impact on Ron's life is such that he has never had a real relationship with a woman. He has suffered chronic depression over many years and has always underachieved and appears to be a very lonely person with no friends. Ron put all this down to the sadistic beatings by Sachisthal who was always down on him. He also remembered all the Charlton officers whom he said were terrible people like Albert Ables and Cecil Boyton.

Ron recalled one time when he was 13; it was during the Christmas break with only six other inmates in the Home. All the other inmates had either gone away with friends of the Home or to camp groups or for a few days with family. Ron was alone in his dormitory and practising his singing: he was in the St Andrew's choir, which was to perform in special Christmas celebrations at the Cathedral in Sydney.

Ron was suddenly aware that others were in the dormitory and as he looked up he could see both Ray Menzies and Norman Sachisthal coming towards him with Menzies grabbing him as he tried to flee. Ron was thrown onto a bed and held down by Menzies as Sachisthal pulled his pants and underwear off. Ron tried his hardest to fight them off, but they were too strong. Held down he was raped by both of them one after the other.

When they were finished Ron dressed quickly and attempted to run from the room but was stopped by Sachisthal who threw him against the wall then thrown on the floor. Sachisthal then kicked him all over the body and disabled Ron when kicked in his private parts. Blood flowed from that area and Sachisthal realised Ron required medical attention. Sachisthal warned Ron not to talk about the sexual assault and said there would be worse problems if he spoke to anyone, especially at the hospital in Camperdown. Half an hour later Ron was being treated as an emergency case.

Some years ago Ron wrote a story of his life, mostly centred on his ten years at Charlton. He showed this to his siblings who read the hundred-page story. They were astounded reading what Ron had gone through as a child. Ron later deleted his story because he had no further use for it.

Ron died in February 2012. He had been waiting for the Court proceedings to commence into the charges he and others made against Albert Ables, alleging sexual offences committed against him by Ables whilst he was an inmate at the Charlton Boys' Home Glebe.

If Ron is looking down, he will know that Ables was sentenced on 22 February 2013 to two years and ten months imprisonment. The Judge Anthony Blackmore took into consideration his age and that there appeared no further problems since 1967 when he was placed on a 12 months good behaviour bond at Dubbo. He was an Officer at the Lillimur Children's Home in Dubbo. Prior to Ron passing on, he told me he had been very traumatised by revisiting old memories that played a great part in destroying his life. He said to me: "I've never been able to socialise and always found it difficult to socialise with women. I could have achieved so much but for Charlton." He was very grateful for my help and the loving caseworkers of Anglicare who I put him in touch with: they made a great difference in his final year.

OLIVER 1950-1954

Oliver was abandoned at two years by his mother. He was passed on from one institution to another. At around ten years of age he was sent to Charlton.

Oliver found Sachisthal's intimidation unbearable, and was always being picked on by him. Sachisthal had some unique punishments, one being with every boy in a large circle around the main hall, running in an anti-clockwise fashion. Sachisthal with a long stick with about one-yard of leather on the end would lash out, hitting very hard the boys he wanted to specifically punish. Should any other innocent boy get hit, then it was too bad. Sadly, during one of these episodes Oliver was struck badly and as he tried to avoid the whip again he fell down, tripping on his own legs and breaking a leg.

After Oliver returned from hospital, Sachisthal in a rage picked up a piece of 4×2 timber and lashed out at him. Oliver, trying to protect himself, put his right arm out and was hit a terrible blow, breaking his wrist. He was later taken back to the hospital.

During his childhood of incarceration, Oliver recalls being sexually assaulted by Cecil Boyton, Alex Whitson and Ray Menzies many times over a long period. Menzies was brutal, sexually hurting Oliver a few times inside the Home at Glebe and also bashing him. Oliver said that Cecil Boyton did it anywhere, even in his green Morris motor car.

Oliver said Sachisthal knew these people were doing these things to the boys of Charlton and has made allegations to the Church that Sachisthal took part in one sexual assault with Menzies in a room off the main dormitory. They both had Oliver give them oral sex.

Oliver remembers other paedophiles such as Bob Davies, the gym instructor, and a Mr Bentley.

Oliver said he still has nightmares about his childhood at Charlton, mainly when he reads of present day paedophile activity or if he watches violent movies where children are hurt. He had never spoken to anyone about his childhood experiences except his wife and me, and later the Anglican Pastoral Care and Professional Standards Unit at St Andrew's in Sydney. He feels he never reached his personal aims in life, has underachieved and has suffered depression over many years. He said he hopes that one day "the sun will shine, and that paedophiles will no longer walk the earth."

Acknowledgements

Often, people like myself simply take friends for granted. I do hope and pray I do not behave in this manner, because of all the things my wonderful grandmother Kate Charlotte Morris nee Carrigg taught me, good manners and how to treat people were the most important.

The Bible teaches us to be kind and loving to each other and never be supercilious, always respectful of how people in our lives put themselves out as friends do.

I pray I never forget the time and effort my good friend Geoff Weir has given to assist me in putting my story together. I cannot count how many times he drove up to trawl through a huge manuscript of well over 400 A4 pages and discuss each item. Geoff engaged the assistance of friends in his "Writing Group". Together they put in long hours discussing and eventually bringing the huge manuscript down to a very easy read, without deleting the true basis of my life story.

The hurt boys like me and others suffered in the Church of England-run Charlton Memorial Home at Glebe was very painful for Geoff Weir and his group, whose names are acknowledged by Geoff elsewhere. I have deliberately made no mention of their names for fear I would miss one.

Acknowledgements

When I first met Geoff, the first thing that I noticed was his keen interest in me and the way, like that of his father, Reverend Ray Weir, his open-armed friendship reached out to me. I contacted Geoff and his sisters Ruth and Jenni as I had taken it upon myself to research the Weir family tree because of my lifelong love for his father.

Ray Weir was the Children's Court Chaplain who first escorted me to Charlton Boys Home. For three years, he was my only outside friend. He always brought a laugh and a smile – Ray Weir's trademark was his beautiful smile – with him into our wretched, downtrodden lives.

I formed an obsession, an imagination of hope that he could be my father, for if I had a choice of a dad, it would be him. When I discovered he had passed away at only 55 years old, I cried, for even after all these years the memory was still present of his love for us Charlton boys. Geoff knows only too well his father had his biological loving family and another, us downtrodden inmates. As I write these words of my love for his father, there are tears falling down my cheek as I recall his regular farewell: 'I'll always be with you'.

Geoff is to me like my beautiful childhood friends, giving of himself as did my lifelong Erskineville friends Ivan Grant, Dave DeBelin and Ken Penning. These three childhood mates were the only people I ever told what they did to me at Yasmar and Charlton. They always helped me and never asked one thing in return.

All my friends are now deceased and I am the last one living. True friends are like diamonds, so rare and precious, and Geoff and his family are always in my prayers. I believe that Geoff has inherited the loving and kind ways of his parents Ray and Audrey Weir.

I would be remiss if I did not mention my loving wife Beryl, who for years supported me while I recalled my dark childhood.

Acknowledgements

It took 47 years before I gained the courage to open up to her, and for years afterwards I would often break down in tears as I helped other former Charlton inmates get assistance, acting as an advocate and more often than not crying on the phone as we relived those terrible days.

I am grateful for the loving efforts of Anglicare workers Phillip Gerber, Jenni Woodhouse and Miriam Stevenson, and the present CEO of Anglicare Pastoral Care, the Reverend Dr Andrew Ford. I cannot forget the prayers for me by the Reverend Joe Zagninski and my present rector, Nigel Fortescue of St Peter's Anglican Church, Campbelltown.

Special thanks to Leonie Sheedy, the CEO of Care Leavers Australian Network (CLAN), and to the Commissioners of the Royal Commission into Institutional Responses to Child Sexual Abuse, especially Justice Jennifer Coates who I know feels our pain.

I would be remiss if I did not thank the former Archbishop of Sydney Peter Jensen and his loving wife Christine, both a tower of strength to men like me who suffered in the failed Church of England homes in my day and years afterwards. So many monsters were in charge of these homes and they, with their paedophile friends, destroyed so many lives. It was so bad that many never got over the physical and sexual pain. A few took suicide as a way out. Peter Jensen has gone well out of his way to ensure future children within the church are protected. His zero tolerance paves the way for the protection of all children. I know truly how much Peter has put in for people like me, I have seen the tears in both Peter and his wife Christine's eyes. Peter Jensen epitomises what the Anglican Church is all about today.

My sincerest thanks to Charlotte Harper and Maria Hawthorne at Editia, who decided my work was worthwhile, and Wendy Dawes who designed the cover. By publishing this book, they have assisted in the fight against sexual offences against children and highlighted how so many of our lives were destroyed. Thank you all very much.

Carl Beauchamp
Sydney, 2016

'A very fortunate life'

Born in Newtown, Sydney, in 1937, the eldest of two sons to Mary and Reginald Beauchamp, Carl Beauchamp was brought up in a dysfunctional household and first put into care in a church home at the age of seven. He spent the rest of his childhood and teenage years in and out of homes where he was abused by those who should have been protecting him.

At 17, Carl started work in the Crago flour mill in Newtown before being called up for compulsory National Service in 1956. After four years in the Citizen Military Forces, he worked two jobs to save for his first home with his sweetheart Beryl, who he married on January 27, 1960.

Carl went into business with his father-in-law, running a cleaning company, and later worked as a foreman at an aluminium company and a supervisor in the bread industry.

A keen and talented sportsman, Carl played rugby league, soccer, golf and tennis. He coached junior soccer teams for many years, building a six-team club, Fairfield Heights, into the largest junior club in Australia at the time with 54 teams.

For 15 years he and Beryl lived in semi-retirement at Tuross Heads on the NSW South Coast, where Carl was active in the community and as secretary of the local branch of the ALP. The

'A very fortunate life'

couple returned to live in Sydney in 2003. They enjoy spending time with their four children, 12 grandchildren, and 17 great-grandchildren.

In 2004, Carl gave evidence about his experiences in the Church of England's Charlton Memorial Home at Glebe to the Senate Affairs References Committee preparing the *Forgotten Australians* and *Protecting Vulnerable Children: A National Challenge* reports. Carl subsequently organised a reunion of former Charlton inmates and encouraged fellow victims to seek support and counselling and put together evidence together for the Royal Commission into Institutional Responses to Child Sexual Abuse.

Carl's strong faith, and his love for Beryl, have sustained him and given him the strength to continue his work as an advocate for other survivors of institutional abuse.